Cinematic Metaphor in Perspective

Cinepoetics

―
Edited by
Hermann Kappelhoff and Michael Wedel

Volume 5

Cinematic Metaphor in Perspective

Reflections on a Transdisciplinary Framework

Edited by
Sarah Greifenstein, Dorothea Horst,
Thomas Scherer, Christina Schmitt,
Hermann Kappelhoff, and Cornelia Müller

DE GRUYTER

ISBN 978-3-11-070910-0
e-ISBN (PDF) 978-3-11-061503-6
e-ISBN (EPUB) 978-3-11-061388-9
ISSN 2569-4294

Disclaimer (figures): All figures were created by the authors, if not indicated otherwise. All screenshots were captured by the authors.

Library of Congress Control Number: 2018951329

Bibliographic information published by the Deutsche Nationalbibliothek
The Deutsche Nationalbibliothek lists this publication in the Deutsche Nationalbibliografie; detailed bibliographic data are available on the Internet at http://dnb.dnb.de.

© 2020 Walter de Gruyter GmbH, Berlin/Boston
This volume is text- and page-identical with the hardback published in 2018.
Cover image: Film still from SPELLBOUND (Alfred Hitchcock, USA 1945)
Typesetting: Integra Software Services Pvt. Ltd.
Printing and binding: CPI books GmbH, Leck

www.degruyter.com

Acknowledgements

The transdisciplinary framework of cinematic metaphor (Müller and Kappelhoff 2018), and the reflections on it in this edited volume, are the outcome of research enabled by *Cinepoetics*, Center for Advanced Film Studies at the Freie Universität Berlin (funded by the German Research Foundation). Within the frame of its first annual theme 'Metaphor – Film Images, Cinematic Thinking, and Cognition' (2015/16), various invited research fellows, project associates, and other visitors to Cinepoetics brought their expertise from different disciplinary backgrounds to colloquia, workshops, and film-analysis sessions. We are grateful for their engaging and inspiring contributions to our work from which we greatly benefited. In particular, we thank our authors Lynne Cameron, Alan Cienki, Anne Eusterschulte, Kathrin Fahlenbrach, Ray Gibbs, and Michael Wedel for their stimulating and enlightening contributions to this edited volume, thereby creating a temporary stabilization in the flow of our process of joint thinking and exchange.

During the biennial conference of the Association for *Researching and Applying Metaphor* (RaAM) that we hosted in Berlin in 2016 with a focus on 'Metaphor in the Arts, in Media and Communication', we had the opportunity to extend the scope of our discussion to an international community of metaphor scholars through a Cinepoetics Roundtable. We thank all participants for their productive questions, comments and reactions.

Beyond being a contributing author, Lynne Cameron took on an important role as a 'book coach' for this edited volume, bringing in her rich academic expertise and providing us with support, inspiration, and motivation during the entire publication process. Thanks to her lucid suggestions and supportive companionship the book project became an exciting and enjoyable joint journey. We are deeply grateful to her for making this journey together with us.

Throughout the publication process, Eileen Rositzka was an extremely helpful and always cheerful adviser accompanying the communication with the publisher. We thank Stella Diedrich and Anna Hofsäß from De Gruyter for their support and advice in preparing the book for publication.

We are grateful to Amber Shields, Mary Hennessy and Lynne Cameron for their meticulous reading and for polishing the English throughout the book.

Without the work of our student assistants Derya Demir, Philine Mayr and Raphael Schotten, the publishing process could not have been realized so smoothly. We gratefully acknowledge their commitment and support in preparing the manuscript for publication.

Berlin, June 2018
Sarah Greifenstein, Dorothea Horst, Thomas Scherer, Christina Schmitt, Hermann Kappelhoff, and Cornelia Müller

Contents

Acknowledgements —— V

Sarah Greifenstein, Dorothea Horst, Thomas Scherer, Christina Schmitt, Hermann Kappelhoff, and Cornelia Müller
Introduction —— 1

Lynne Cameron
**From Metaphor to Metaphorizing:
How Cinematic Metaphor Opens Up Metaphor Studies —— 17**

Michael Wedel
**Murnau and Metaphor:
From Cinematic Expressionism to Cinematic Expressive Movements —— 36**

Alan Cienki
**Insights for Linguistics and Gesture Studies from Film Studies:
A View from Researching Cinematic Metaphor —— 53**

Kathrin Fahlenbrach
**Moving Metaphors:
Affects, Movements, and Embodied Metaphors in Cinema —— 69**

Anne Eusterschulte
Actio per distans:
Blumenberg's Metaphorology and Hitchcock's REAR WINDOW —— 93

Raymond W. Gibbs, Jr.
Our Metaphorical Experiences of Film —— 120

Name Index —— 141

Subject Index —— 144

About the Authors —— 146

About the Editors —— 149

Sarah Greifenstein, Dorothea Horst, Thomas Scherer,
Christina Schmitt, Hermann Kappelhoff, and Cornelia Müller

Introduction

What is cinematic metaphor?

What distinguishes interdisciplinary from transdisciplinary work is what separates a simile from a metaphor. Both interdisciplinarity and simile place their two benchmarks side by side, as separate and distinct, and, on this basis, suggest similarity or comparability. Transdisciplinarity and metaphor on the other hand, remove their referential realms from such a self-contained state and bring them together with the result that the two compose something new, something shared that is more than the sum of its previous parts. Both referential realms give up their isolation and self-containedness in order to come together into existence as something third through an experiencing and understanding in terms of the other.

As a transdisciplinary theoretical and methodological approach, *Cinematic Metaphor* emerged and developed from a collaboration between film studies and linguistic metaphor research along with integrative exchanges on different disciplinary perspectives at *Cinepoetics*, Center for Advanced Film Studies at the Freie Universität Berlin. The monograph of Müller, Kappelhoff, and colleagues – *Cinematic Metaphor. Experience – Affectivity – Temporality* (2018) – is the outcome of this longstanding work and of numerous fruitful discussions on metaphor in audiovisual media and face-to-face interaction. Starting from the media-character of audiovisual images as *cinematic movement-images* rather than as 'moving images', the book develops a theoretical and methodological framework for metaphor in audiovisual media as performative action which is grounded in the dynamics of viewers' embodied intersubjective experiences with film.

This framework constitutes the key reference for this edited volume, *Cinematic Metaphor in Perspective. Reflections on a Transdisciplinary Framework* with contributions from applied and cognitive linguistics, film and media studies, media history, philosophy, and psychology. As a companion volume to *Cinematic Metaphor. Experience – Affectivity – Temporality*, it addresses the transdisciplinary exchange on cinematic metaphor that has both set the stage for its emergence and advanced its further development over the past ten years. The contributing scholars explore how the framework of cinematic metaphor inspires their views of metaphor in film and of metaphor theory and analysis more generally. In this light, the essays of this edited volume provide insight into the contributors' (transdisciplinary, metaphorical) process of experiencing and understanding their research area in terms of cinematic metaphor or, as Max Black has described it, into "a world seen from certain perspective" (Black 1993 [1977], 38), thereby creating new realities.

An alternative approach to the analysis of audiovisual media

What is the necessity for, and added value of, a new perspective on metaphors in film, television, and video, given the range of existing cognitive media studies (e.g., Coëgnarts and Kravanja 2015), cognitive-linguistic (e.g., Forceville and Urios-Aparisi 2009), and multimodal research (e.g., Wildfeuer and Bateman 2017) in the field of audiovisual media? The crucial theoretical and empirical starting point, and key argument for the framework of cinematic metaphor, is the media specificity of audiovisual images as movement-images, not as moving pictures representing content. That is why the notions of "audiovisual metaphor" (Fahlenbrach 2010, this volume, Whittock 1990) or "multimodal metaphor" (e.g., Forceville 2009) that take metaphor in language as a reference point and, furthermore, consider audiovisual images to consist of accumulated articulatory modes 'representing' moving content, reach their limits when it comes to the dynamics of the cinematic movement-image (Deleuze 2008 [1983]). The term movement-image refers to the specific mode of perception that unfolds temporally and experientially along viewers' processes of film-viewing and thereby orchestrates their processes of meaning-making. As such an aesthetic and logical framing, the movement-image constitutes a fundamental principle – a media mode of experience – that is shared by audiovisual images, in whatever form, more generally. Cinematic metaphors emerge with this movement experience of film-viewing, rather than from represented content or narratives that cognitive media studies of metaphors and multimodal metaphor analyses of audiovisual media take for granted.

Along with starting from the media character of the cinematic as the embodied experiential grounds for the emergence of metaphorical meaning comes a counter position to the idea of a sender-receiver model of communication. Cinematic metaphor is considered to be created, to be 'done' by spectators in their embodied processes of cinematic perception. It is this understanding of metaphorical meaning-making as performative action, as 'work' that spectators are doing over the course of viewing, that is labeled "the poiesis of film-viewing" (Müller and Kappelhoff 2018, Chapter 1.4.) and that characterizes cinematic experience. In this light, cinematic metaphor differs fundamentally from most cognitive-linguistic, cognitive media studies, and multimodal approaches to metaphor in audiovisual media that conceive of film-viewing as a specific form of information processing and thereby conceptualize film viewers as rather passive 'unpackers' of messages 'intentionally' designed by a producer.

It is in this sense that cinematic metaphor opens up an alternative perspective on meaning-making processes in audiovisual media and beyond. In the next section of this introductory chapter, we give a brief overview of the fundamental film and media-theoretical assumptions for the framework of cinematic metaphor and explain how it also applies to face-to-face communication. Subsequently, and by analogy with *Cinematic Metaphor. Experience – Affectivity – Temporality*, we zoom in on three key characteristics of cinematic metaphor – experience, affectivity, and temporality – and then illustrate the theoretical outline of cinematic metaphor with a brief analysis of a German TV commercial from the DIY supermarket Hornbach.

A theoretical framework based on the media-character of audiovisual images

Introducing cinematic metaphor as an alternative approach implies a close examination and classification of contemporary metaphor research. In this regard, two major positions mark opposing views and traditions in the field of metaphor research: George Lakoff and Mark Johnson's cognitively informed conceptual metaphor theory, and Hans Blumenberg's philosophical metaphorology. The two approaches differ fundamentally in their answer to the question of what is the nature of 'thinking' and how meaning is being constructed. While the (neuro-) cognitive approach considers meaning to be rooted in universal cognitive schemata, philosophical metaphor theory locates it within a historical-cultural horizon. Developing the framework of cinematic metaphor from the media-character of audiovisual images, as a mode of experience that orchestrates viewers' perceptual and meaning-making processes in a situated manner, necessarily entails taking the historicity of metaphorical meaning-making into consideration. Otherwise, this concrete situatedness of meaning gets lost in favor of universal hard-wired cognitive structures.

With a rhetoric-based position to metaphors in audiovision (especially Blumenberg's metaphorology and Friedrich Nietzsche's philosophy of rhetoric), cinematic metaphor is elaborated as emerging within and from the media mode of perception, i.e., from the spectator's experiencing of movement-images. Such a 'doing' (see also Gibbs 2017, Jensen 2017) of metaphor as evolving from the concrete sensing of the film and creating new, fragile realities is in line with Lakoff and Johnson's early formulation of metaphors as multidimensional experiential gestalts (Lakoff and Johnson 1980), and Max Black's idea of metaphors as cognitive instruments (Black 1993 [1977]). In this sense, metaphors are not conceived of as reproducing existing cognitive schemas or a given reality (whatever that might be). On the contrary, they develop, form, model, and transform the conceptual systems that constitute our reality and create a commonly shared scope of different experiential perspectives through the principle of experiencing and understanding one kind of thing in terms of another. Cinematic metaphor thus resonates with dynamic approaches to metaphor in discourse (Cameron 2011, Müller 2008a, b) that have underlined its situatedness, ephemerality, always changing nature in producing a shared meaning of what counts as 'real' when a self-evident reality is not available.

'Doing' metaphor (both in face-to-face communication and) in film-viewing emerges within and from viewers' reflexive feeling for their entanglement[1] with the surrounding reality, i.e., their perceiving and sensing of the film. It happens as they are entangled affectively with the unfolding of cinematic movement-images, captured by the concept of 'cinematic expressive movement' (Kappelhoff 2004). Such a reciprocal relation in which the film is being bodily realized as the expression of another subjectivity is inextricably linked with a phenomenological concept of intersubjectivity. Following Vivian Sobchack's influential neo-phenomenological film theory, any movement occurring in the audiovisual composition materializes outside the screen as bodily sensation in the viewer, i.e. is embodied by that viewer. The spectator understands the film as an individually sensed experience of another body, the world of an unfamiliar, other 'I' that becomes a concrete experience in his or her own body, or as "expression of experience by experience", (Merleau-Ponty 1968 [1964], 155, quoted in Sobchack 1992, 3). Such a phenomenological understanding of the cinematic mode of experience as intersubjective, reflexive, and dynamic interaction resonates with Lakoff and Johnson's formula of metaphor as "understanding and experiencing one kind of thing in terms of another" (Lakoff and Johnson 1980, 5) and strongly contrasts with the model of cognitive film and metaphor theories in which of embodiment is seen as physiologically grounded, shared, meaningful reality which is assumed to exist prior to any communicative situation.

Summing up the basic theoretical assumptions of cinematic metaphor:
- Cinematic metaphors emerge from movement-images, not from moving pictures. Movement-images constitute a specific mode of experience that characterizes various genres and media formats of audiovisual images and provides the ground for cinematic metaphors to emerge.

---

[1] Entanglement is used terminologically here. It translates the German "Verwickelt-Sein" and, along with the weaker terms 'involvement', 'being engaged with', seeks to capture the idea of being enmeshed in a film affectively and cognitively. Escape is possible, but would mean missing the film.

- Cinematic metaphors are dynamic connections between different experiential domains that evolve from the aesthetics of the film's expressivity. This expressivity is realized as the viewer's own affective experience, and at the same time as distinct from a mode of experience of another subjectivity.
- In this sense, neither cinematic images nor cinematic metaphors solely reproduce existing cognitive schemas of movement, space, and time. Instead, they create new differences and modalities, i.e., new 'realities', in a concrete, historically situated manner.
- Cinematic metaphors are 'done' by the spectators who create new links between different modes of experience in the act of viewing films. This process can be described as an artistic production, a poiesis of film-viewing.

Having outlined the theoretical framework of cinematic metaphor on the basis of the media-character of audiovisual images, we now demonstrate its fundamental parallels to processes of metaphorical meaning-making in multimodal face-to-face interaction before proceeding to illustrate three cornerstones of cinematic metaphor: experience, affectivity, and temporality.

What face-to-face interaction shares with film-viewing

Meaning-making processes as we understand them within the framework of cinematic metaphor provide an interface to face-to-face interaction. What face-to-face interaction shares with film-viewing is that both are temporal forms of experiencing and interaffective engagement from which metaphor emerges as a dynamic process rather than as a static feature (Cameron 2011, Müller 2008a). Interlocutors in a conversation as much as film viewers are reflexively affected by the expressivity of another subjectivity. This subjectivity is realized as their own physical experience, and likewise as distinct from another subjectivity's mode of experience. Indeed, such a reflexive understanding of human expressivity became a role model for cinematic expressivity informing film theory from its very beginning (Kappelhoff 2004).

Interactive movement is a key element for such reflexive affection. While cinematic expressivity is staged through audiovisual modalities, such as camera movement, sound design, or montage, human expressivity emanates on the level of hands, head, legs, arms, and trunk movements, together with the prosodic contours of speech. These interactive movements compose to expressive multimodal gestalts as co-participants are speaking and gesturing with one another in the flow of discourse. Metaphors emerge, unfold, and change within this interaffective temporal flow as a dynamic process; they are 'done' by interlocutors in ever changing transfers. In this light, the three key characteristics of cinematic metaphor to be outlined in the following sections also apply to metaphorical meaning beyond audiovisual media, pointing to fundamental properties of multimodal face-to-face interaction.

Cinematic metaphor and experience

Experience is a key characteristic of cinematic metaphor. By taking the mediality of audiovisual images as movement-images as vantage point, the process of film-viewing itself constitutes a metaphorical process of "experiencing and understanding one kind of thing in terms of another": a process of interaction between spectator and film that is characterized by intersubjectivity and reflexive awareness of another subject position and of a situated context. Cinematic metaphor is a 'doing' that resides in this intersubjective, reflexive, and temporally-structured experience embodied by the viewer.

With such a concept of embodiment, the notion of cinematic metaphor differs from the common cognitive-science understanding. Embodiment and with it metaphorical meaning are not considered to reside in universal perceptual schemata; they are inseparable from concrete moments of experience. This local anchoring in the here and now of a communicative encounter is one of the dimensions that multimodal face-to-face interaction shares with the poiesis of film-viewing.

In the light of such a phenomenological understanding of embodied experience, metaphoricity is not statically instantiated but dynamically created from the media-specific mode of perception across different audiovisual forms. The aesthetic orchestration of the unfolding movement-images intertwines with the affective experiences of viewers, and grounds figurative meaning.

Cinematic metaphor and affectivity

In the process of viewing a film, spectators are entangled with the dynamics of cinematic movement-images that come with a particular movement quality: an affective quality. Cinematic metaphor emerges from that affective experience. The key concept that allows to describe the process of film-viewing in its affective dynamics is the notion of expressive movement. It is historically rooted in the aesthetic strategies of affect modulation, developed within the concept of melodrama in theatre and film (Kappelhoff 2004).

With its focus on the aesthetics of movement, expressive movement describes a fundamental trait not only of film but also of human gestures: their movement qualities as a form of expressivity that modulates affective experiences. This theoretical parallelism between body movement and cinematic movement expressed by the notion of movement-image also applies to metaphorical meaning-making. Metaphoricity is inseparable from speakers' and spectators' affective entanglement with gestural and cinematic movement.

Based on a phenomenological understanding of embodied experience, an understanding of affect becomes evident that takes a counter position to an idea of distinct and static emotions. Affect is considered to result from the temporal staging of film's expressive means as it organizes the perceptual processes of spectators dynamically. These affective experiences provide the aesthetic grounding for the emergence of metaphorical meaning. Cinematic expressive movement applies as a methodological tool to analyze processes of affect modulation and metaphorical meaning-making through cinematic composition across various audiovisual forms, be they shorter ones like television news or longer ones like feature films.

Cinematic metaphor and temporality

The poiesis of film-viewing cannot be considered without recourse to the temporal structure of cinematic images, of audiovisual media, and of embodied experience in general. In the process of viewing, spectators experience a temporal flow of audiovisual composition. They go through an affective parcours of cinematic experience within and from which they 'do' metaphors. It is in this sense that cinematic metaphor is inherently procedural and it shares this characteristic with metaphor in multimodal interaction. Metaphorical meaning emerges in processes of making sense, of striving for intersubjectivity, bounded to the flow of talking and gesturing, of watching and listening.

The temporality of cinematic metaphor affects all levels of cinematic staging, from small units of cinematic expressivity to the flow of an entire film. Metaphors can emerge on micro levels and successively unfold and develop metaphorical scenarios on a meso level of temporal orchestration that structure, for example, particular stretches of discourse or film. Metaphorical scenarios can evolve into metaphorical themes running through the macro level of entire feature films, political reports in television, or a face-to-face interaction and thus form systematic metaphors in Lynne Cameron's sense (2008). In this light, metaphorical meaning-making becomes evident as a temporal process unfolding on different layers and different time scales, constantly changing along the procedural experience of film-viewing.

In the following, the framework of cinematic metaphor with its three key characteristics is illustrated with a brief analysis of a German TV commercial from the DIY supermarket Hornbach. Over the course of watching the commercial, a cinematic metaphor emerges that orchestrates a feeling for an unfinished DIY project in terms of something incessantly following us until it is finished (off).

Finish it. Before it finishes you off: Cinematic metaphor in a television commercial

The commercial was produced in 2007 (director: Carl Erik Rinsch, advertising agency: Heimat) within the context of a promotional campaign for the DIY supermarket Hornbach under the slogan "Finish it. Before it finishes you off" [*Mach es fertig, bevor es dich fertig macht*],[2] addressing DIY projects for which the client company offers to provide the necessary tools.[3] Over the course of one minute, the commercial stages the relationship between a man and his old bathroom as an experience of being haunted, which becomes the vehicle for the metaphor topic: the man's state of mind in view of a neglected home improvement project.

The commercial begins by showing a man leaving a flat on his way to his desk job. Slowly, without body tension and with a lowered gaze, he walks down the corridor. When he turns his head slightly to the side, a bathroom with an open toilet bowl, an ancient claw-foot bathtub with a huge old boiler above and a bath mat shaped like a huge foot in front of it come into view. This aged and filthy bath strongly contrasts with the rest of the rather elegant and well-arranged flat as far as we have seen it before. On the soundtrack as well a contrast dominates: a melancholic theme collides with sound closeups of bubbling, hissing and splashing noises. In what follows, this neglected bathroom 'comes to life': in the shape of an open brickwork walking on two legs in a sort-of upright position, it follows the man down the street on his way to work with muffled, reverberating steps. By sharing the same slow and heavy walking rhythm which leaves an acoustic trace, i.e., loud and dull reverberating steps, the man and his animated bathroom are related to one another; they are perceived as being one. From this cinematic perceptual experience, a scenario of 'being followed' emerges (Figure 1).

---

2 Here as well as in the following, German originals are given in italics and square brackets.
3 For an extended version of the analysis see Schmitt 2015 and forthcoming/2019. The version for this book was prepared by Christina Schmitt and Dorothea Horst.

Figure 1: Visual relation and synchronized rhythms creating a scenario of 'being followed' (MACH ES FERTIG, 2007).

This relation between the man and his bathroom transforms more and more into a hunting and fleeing scenario, especially through the fast rolling and jumping movements and howling sounds 'made' by the bathroom. The string theme becomes more dramatic and is disrupted through dull clonking and metallic banging attributed to the animated bath. It appears as a huge animal-like figure relentlessly following the man, hunting and stalking him through empty streets. However, this stalking is not primarily threatening. With the sad and melancholic rather than aggressive noise of the howling, the bathroom is perceived as something that needs attention, just like a neglected dog demanding its master's attention.

Again and again we see partial turning movements of the man towards his stalking bathroom, while the dynamics of the initially slow and heavy walking movement intensifies, becoming turbulent and chaotic. Various changing perspectives and movement directions, e.g., away and towards the camera, accelerated movements of the bathroom and the man, and an increased cutting rate, as well as the noises swallowing the music, create a movement experience of escalation and thus push the hunting scenario towards a peak. Then, the man is shown from behind, finally facing the bathroom completely, before he attacks his follower with a shrill noise that had been previously established as the sound evoked by the bathroom's movement. Now, it is no longer a relation between a hunter and somebody being hunted, but a confrontation, a battle in which a series of slow-motion shots is edited in fast sequence, thus deconstructing both figures and merging them into one (Figure 2).

Figure 2: A following and hunting transforms into a fight that is finally resolved (MACH ES FERTIG, 2007).

With a cut, the action space changes abruptly from the gloomy beige street into a bright, crisp, and calm modernized bathroom. The previous noise as well as the experience of a highly dynamic, downright chaotic and tense movement have faded away. A static long-shot shows the man – now wearing jeans and t-shirt instead of a suit – fastening a shower head in the middle of his now renovated bathroom that has changed back into an inanimate thing. The spot ends with a voice-over saying "Finish it. Before it finishes you off" [*Mach es fertig. Bevor es dich fertig macht*] and a fade-in of Hornbach's corporate slogan "There is always something to be done." [*Es gibt immer was zu tun.*] (Figure 2).

It is only at the very end, with hearing the concluding slogan and seeing the brand's logo and corporate slogan, that language comes into play. Nevertheless, right from the beginning of the spot a play with language is taking place. Several German idioms, all dealing with mental states in terms of physical ones, are subtly called up through the temporal orchestration of audiovisual staging that viewers are entangled with in their process of viewing. Apart from the already mentioned "being followed or haunted by something at every turn" [*auf Schritt und Tritt von etwas verfolgt werden*], the temporal aesthetics of the commercial activate the experiential realms (Müller 2008a) of "to face a problem or a challenge" [*sich einer Herausforderung/einem Problem stellen*], "to attack a task" [*etwas in Angriff nehmen*], or "going loopy" [*durchdrehen*]. In this light, the movement pattern of a heavy and at once weakened dynamic that intensifies and gets more and more chaotic until fading out that orchestrates the entire commercial, figures as the dynamic image of mental states. The shown diegetic exterior space (the flat, the street, etc.) transforms in the process of film-viewing so that the emerging actual action space is retrospectively revealed as an inner life ascribed to the man: an image of being depressed and haunted, being threatened with the danger of going crazy that is only resolved in the end.

The utterance of the voice-over, "Finish it. Before it finishes you off" [*Mach es fertig, bevor es dich fertig macht*] relates both to this feeling of being haunted and to the audiovisual representation of the ageing bathroom. "Finish it" is congruent with what we see: fixing the shower head, the man obviously finishes the renovation of his bathroom. At the same time, with the fading-out of the previous chaotic movement we experience him as finally overcoming the previously animated bathroom that was hunting him, by, as it were, wringing its neck. Now the bathroom, with its cool and bluish white appearance, is inanimate and rather dead. The second part of the utterance, "Before it finishes you off", connects with the former physical life-or-death struggle that can only have one winner. At the same time, it emphasizes the commercial's topic of a hunted man's physical and mental exhaustion; an exhaustion that results from being haunted by incessantly thinking of a neglected, still unfinished home improvement project. In this regard, the voice-over slogan puts straight what has been unfolding as an embodied experience of the commercial's temporal aesthetics: *a feeling of restlessness and exhaustion through a heavy and weakened dynamic that intensifies and gets more and more chaotic until finally coming to rest.*

Through viewers' experiencing of the commercial's movement-images, a highly complex cinematic metaphor has emerged. Only within and through this experiential, affective, and temporal process do we come to a specific understanding of an unfinished process: we create and embody a fictional world, in which a man becomes insane due to a paranoid imagining of his old-fashioned bathroom transforming into a monster and chasing him through the streets, until he finally decides to fight with it in order to overcome his phantasm.

Reflections on cinematic metaphor: Overview of the contributions

Cinematic Metaphor as a topic and outcome of transdisciplinary research came to life from the very beginning of *Cinepoetics*, Center for Advanced Film Studies at Freie Universität Berlin. In 2015/16, the first annual theme was 'Metaphor – Film Images, Cinematic Thinking, and Cognition' (under the leadership of Cornelia Müller, together with Hermann Kappelhoff and Michael Wedel). In colloquia, workshops, and film-analysis sessions, we engaged in a substantial discussion of various disciplinary approaches with different theoretical assumptions and traditions, from different academic realms of discourse.[4] An early endeavour to widen the realm of our discussion into the scientific community was the Cinepoetics roundtable at 'RaAM 11: Metaphor in the Arts, in Media and Communication' – the biannual conference for researching and applying metaphor – held at Freie Universität Berlin and European University Viadrina (Frankfurt/Oder).[5]

This book, as well as its companion volume *Cinematic Metaphor. Experience – Affectivity – Temporality* (Müller and Kappelhoff 2018), are manifestations of this thinking in progress, temporary stabilizations in the ongoing process of reflecting on and with metaphor and audiovisual media. The authors contributing to this book – **Lynne Cameron** (Applied Linguistics, Professor Emerita, Open University, UK), **Alan Cienki** (Cognitive Linguistics, VU Universiteit Amsterdam, NL, and Moscow State Linguistic University, RUS), **Anne Eusterschulte** (Philosophy, Freie Universität Berlin, GER), **Kathrin Fahlenbrach** (Film and Media Studies, Universität Hamburg, GER), **Raymond W. Gibbs, Jr.** (Psychology, Professor Emeritus, UC Santa Cruz, CA, US) and **Michael Wedel** (Film and Media Studies, Filmuniversität Potsdam KONRAD WOLF and co-director of *Cinepoetics*, Center for Advanced Film Studies at Freie Universität Berlin, GER) – were key participants of these exchanges. Over the course of the year creating a common language to initiate a productive exchange between the different approaches was the main goal: a language through which the thoughts of, e.g., George Lakoff, Mark Johnson, Hans Blumenberg, Vivian Sobchack, Max Black, or Lynne Cameron, and films by Alfred Hitchcock, Ruth Lingford, Tom Tykwer, William Wyler and others could be related to one another. We considered these discussions not as a joint wrap-up or evaluation, but as initiation of an inter- and transdisciplinary discussion on a larger scale.

The reflections on the concept of *cinematic metaphor* at the heart of this book are not final remarks set in stone but temporary stabilizations of the ongoing discussion on metaphorical meaning-making and cinematic thinking. Across the

---

4 These discussions draw on the work of the research project 'Multimodal Metaphor and Expressive Movement' (2009–2013), a collaboration between film studies (Hermann Kappelhoff) and linguistic metaphor research (Cornelia Müller) at the interdisciplinary research center Languages of Emotion at the Freie Universität Berlin. The editors of this book were all members of this project.
5 With its issue 'Metaphor in the Arts, in Media and Communication' the second volume of the open-access online journal *Mediaesthetics* (2017) is the follow-up publication to the RaAM 11 conference, including contributions from philosophy (Petra Gehring), architecture (José Mario Gutierrez Marquez) and film studies (Jennifer M. Barker). See http://www.mediaesthetics.org/index.php/mae/issue/view/10/showToc

volume many different formats come together: applications, critiques, transferals. A multivoicedness that we consider to be essential for a transdisciplinary discussion.

In her chapter 'From Metaphor to Metaphorizing: How Cinematic Metaphor Opens Up Metaphor Studies', **Lynne Cameron** argues that the book *Cinematic Metaphor* has the potential for wider application to the study of metaphor in human life. Close analysis and theorizing of metaphor in film prompts Cameron to (re)consider what is entailed by regarding discourse and film-viewing as flow, and examining metaphorizing – rather than metaphor – in this flow. Various types of metaphorizing are discussed, including the creative processes of poets and film-makers in which Vehicles offer themselves for connecting with Topics. With an analysis of a coaching conversation, Cameron highlights the shifting, evolving nature of trajectories of systematic metaphors. Moreover, she discusses methodological issues in extracting these trajectories from data, especially reflecting on the problems with the conventional 'A IS B' formulation of metaphors. From a perspective of metaphorizing as flow, she introduces a new connecting symbol, the tilde, for the labelling of metaphors, and reverses the order of Vehicle and Topic: $V \sim T \to M_{ing}$.

Michael Wedel's contribution on 'Murnau and Metaphor: From Cinematic Expressionism to Cinematic Expressive Movements' investigates the film-historical and film-theoretical classification of Weimar art cinema and German expressionist film as exhibiting an overall allegorical mode of cinematic representation and storytelling. Starting from film-theoretical appropriations of literary figurativity, e.g., by Roman Jakobson or Christian Metz, he offers a critical review of the rather static structuralist view that considers cinematic metaphoricity as occasional irritation and calculated interruption in the discursive and narrative economy of filmic signification. Wedel contrasts this traditional perspective with reflections on the new theoretical approach of Cinematic Metaphor and especially one of its core concepts – cinematic expressive movement. By analyzing various shadow play sequences in Wilhelm Murnau's SCHLOSS VOGELÖD and NOSFERATU, he shows that instead of being erratic stylistic imprints, these sequences come into view as parts of ongoing affective modulation and meaning-making along which Murnau's films take their spectators. Based on these exemplary analyses, Wedel envisions a reconstruction of the signature of Weimar cinema's historicity from a renewed perspective that goes beyond the formula of expressionism and across individual oeuvres and genres.

In his contribution, **Alan Cienki** gives 'Insights for Linguistics and Gesture Studies From Film Studies: A View From Researching Cinematic Metaphor'. Starting from the inherent dynamicity of metaphor in cinema, he reflects on its applicability to language use in face-to-face interaction, particularly processes of meaning-making and how they can be analyzed and interpreted. In this light, he moreover argues the case for considering the poetics of everyday practices. An overview of recent approaches demonstrates that considering co-verbal gestures provides a more complete picture of complex temporal structures and how language reflects aspects of speakers' conceptualizations, not least due to gestures' potential of making the abstract tangible. Cienki's examination of the aesthetic dimension of gestures – this is what he considers the poetics of everyday behavior – leads him to argue for a more balanced position of cognitive linguistics between the humanities and social sciences by giving aesthetic attention to the phenomena under examination in empirical research.

In 'Moving Metaphors: Affects, Movements, and Embodied Metaphors in Cinema', **Kathrin Fahlenbrach** takes up the interdisciplinary exchange with a critical reading of papers on cinematic expressive movements by Kappelhoff, Müller, and colleagues, and the phenomenologically-oriented concept of cinematic metaphor building upon it. Fahlenbrach puts alongside this concept a cognitivist approach to audiovisual metaphors and embodied meanings in moving images. With an analysis of Tom Tykwer's LOLA RENNT [RUN LOLA RUN], she explores the compatibility as well as the differences of these two perspectives. In particular, she underlines the role of cognitive schemata and stereotypes that she considers to be relevant for metaphorical meaning-making in audiovisual media. Fahlenbrach emphasizes the necessity and productivity of mutual exchange – highlighting how phenomenologically-informed and cognitivist approaches can raise each other's awareness for different aspects of film experience and understanding.

With **Anne Eusterschulte's** contribution '*Actio per distans*. Blumenberg's Metaphorology and Hitchcock's REAR WINDOW', one of the most important German traditions of philosophical metaphor theory comes into focus. Eusterschulte gives an introduction to Hans Blumenberg's pragmatic and cultural-historical understanding of metaphor and reflects on its implications for the poiesis of film-viewing. In her analysis of a metaphorical complex in REAR WINDOW, she describes how the film stages manifold window situations in such a manner that modes of viewing experiences intertwine with modes of temporality. She suggests that these intertwined stagings are what viewers of the film, in an affective involvement and free play of imagination, think with concerning transitory threshold situations. Eusterschulte concludes that in order to become aware of the poiesis of realities in film-viewing, its potentialities, and eventualities, an occasionally criminological sense and a distant vantage point are necessary, a fundamental principle that Blumenberg has called 'actio per distans'.

'Our Metaphorical Experiences of Films' are, as **Raymond W. Gibbs, Jr.** points out in his contribution, shaped by the temporality of movement-images – from dynamics unfolding within a single scene to metaphorical themes that emerge over the course of a whole film. He illustrates this with an in-depth analysis of Alfred Hitchcock's SPELLBOUND. Gibbs offers an account of how spectators construct complex metaphorical impressions and meanings during and after film-viewing with their whole body through 'embodied simulation' processes. Combining findings from psycholinguistics and cognitive sciences with the film-studies informed concept of cinematic metaphor, Gibbs elaborates how viewers experience film through sensory and embodied processes. In this light, they literally feel 'moved' by a film because of audiovisual movement patterns that lead to embodied simulation processes. According to Gibbs, films 'push their audience around' in elaborate ways with affective movement experiences (that differ from those of real world events), immersing viewers in film worlds. As a result, by being bodily perceived as movements, metaphorical experiences are likewise inherently affective. Gibbs concludes by suggesting that such embodied processes of meaning-making extend metaphors in audiovisual media.

The relation between this edited volume and its close companion *Cinematic Metaphor* (2018) is a manifestation of an ongoing exchange of thinking between and across disciplines. Not least by referring to the analyses and examples of others and (critically) reflecting on them, developing them further, and entering into a dialog with the theoretical assumptions, a further step towards joint transdisciplinary thinking is done.

Audiovisual sources

LOLA RENNT [RUN LOLA RUN], Dir. Tom Tykwer, X-Filme, GER 1998.
MACH ES FERTIG, BEVOR ES DICH FERTIG MACHT – BADEZIMMER [FINISH IT. BEFORE IT FINISHES YOU OFF – BATHROOM], Dir. Carl Erik Rinsch (Heimat) for Hornbach, GER 2007.
NOSFERATU – EINE SYMPHONIE DES GRAUENS [NOSFERATU]. Dir. Friedrich Wilhelm Murnau. Prana-Film, GER 1922.
REAR WINDOW, Dir. Alfred Hitchcock, Paramount, USA 1954.
SCHLOSS VOGELÖD [THE HAUNTED CASTLE]. Dir. Friedrich Wilhelm Murnau. Uco-Film, GER 1921.
SPELLBOUND, Dir. Alfred Hitchcock, Selznick International Pictures, USA 1945.

Bibliography

Black, Max. 1993. "More about Metaphor." In *Metaphor and Thought*, edited by Andrew Ortony, 19–41. Cambridge: Cambridge University Press. Original edition 1977.
Cameron, Lynne. 2008. "Metaphor and Talk." In *The Cambridge Handbook of Metaphor and Thought*, edited by Raymond W. Jr. Gibbs, 197–211. Cambridge: Cambridge University Press.

Cameron, Lynne. 2011. *Metaphor and Reconciliation. The Discourse Dynamics of Empathy in Post-Conflict Conversations*, Routledge Studies in Linguistics. New York, NY: Routledge.
Coëgnarts, Maarten, and Peter Kravanja, eds. 2015. *Embodied Cognition and Cinema*. Leuven: Leuven University Press.
Deleuze, Gilles. 2008. *Cinema 1. The Movement Image*. London: Continuum. Original edition 1983.
Fahlenbrach, Kathrin. 2010. *Audiovisuelle Metaphern. Zur Körper- und Affektästhetik in Film und Fernsehen*. Marburg: Schüren.
Forceville, Charles. 2009. "Non-Verbal and Multimodal Metaphor in a Cognitivist Framework. Agendas for Research." In *Multimodal Metaphor*, edited by Charles Forceville and Eduardo Urios-Aparisi. Berlin/Boston, MA: Walter de Gruyter.
Forceville, Charles, and Eduardo Urios-Aparisi, eds. 2009. *Multimodal Metaphor*. Berlin: Mouton de Gruyter.
Gibbs, Raymond W. Jr. 2017. "Metaphor and Human Experience." RaAM. Specialized Seminar: Ecological Cognition and Metaphor, Odense, Denmark, 18–19 May.
Jensen, Thomas Wiben. 2017. "Doing Metaphor: An Ecological Perspective on Metaphoricity in Discourse." In *Metaphor. Embodied Cognition and Discourse*, edited by Beate Hampe, 257–276. Cambridge: Cambridge University Press.
Kappelhoff, Hermann. 2004. *Matrix der Gefühle. Das Kino, das Melodrama und das Theater der Empfindsamkeit*. Berlin: Vorwerk 8.
Lakoff, George, and Mark Johnson. 1980. *Metaphors We Live By*. Chicago, IL: University of Chicago Press.
Merleau-Ponty, Maurice. 1968. *The Visible and the Invisible*. Evanston, IL: Northwestern University Press. Original edition 1964.
Müller, Cornelia. 2008a. *Metaphors Dead and Alive, Sleeping and Waking. A Dynamic View*. Chicago, IL: University of Chicago Press.
Müller, Cornelia. 2008b. "What Gestures Reveal About the Nature of Metaphor." In *Metaphor and Gesture*, edited by Alan Cienki and Cornelia Müller, 219–245. Amsterdam: John Benjamins.
Müller, Cornelia, and Hermann Kappelhoff. 2018. *Cinematic Metaphor. Experience – Affectivity – Temporality*. In collaboration with Sarah Greifenstein, Dorothea Horst, Thomas Scherer, and Christina Schmitt. Berlin/Boston, MA: Walter de Gruyter.
Schmitt, Christina, and Matthias Grotkopp, eds. 2017. *Mediaesthetics Vol. 2: Metaphor in the Arts, in Media and Communication*. Berlin: Cinepoetics. www.mediaesthetics.org.
Sobchack, Vivian. 1992. *The Address of the Eye. A Phenomenology of Film Experience*. Princeton, NJ: Princeton University.
Whittock, Trevor. 1990. *Metaphor and Film*. Cambridge: Cambridge University Press.
Wildfeuer, Janina, and John Bateman. 2017. *Film Text Analysis. New Perspectives on the Analysis of Filmic Meaning*. New York, NY: Routledge, Taylor & Francis Group.

Lynne Cameron
From Metaphor to Metaphorizing: How Cinematic Metaphor Opens Up Metaphor Studies

Introduction

When I started working on metaphor, my older son was eight years old and his brother was six. Their fascination with metaphor and their ability to grasp the idea of metaphor and discuss examples with me all contradicted existing theory and highlighted the absence of evidence on how children understand metaphor. Addressing this gap led me to classroom discourse studies, where I began building an analytic methodology for metaphor in talk and the theoretical framework to support it. In the process, I had to question assumptions then rampant in the field that downgraded metaphor in actual discourse to 'mere instantiation' of 'A IS B' conceptual metaphor.

Time has passed and I am writing this chapter while my new granddaughter naps after another sleepless night for that same older son and his wife. We walk around in a zombie-like state, snatching moments of clarity out of a fog of tiredness in which to work. In a reflective mood, and with a renewed vigor prompted by *Cinematic Metaphor. Experience – Affectivity – Temporality* (2018), I return here to issues in metaphor theory that continue to puzzle and irritate.

Müller, Kappelhoff and colleagues demonstrate how important it is for cinematic metaphor studies to consider film 'in its own right', with its full, multimodal range of technological effects and its production and spectator history of making and viewing, rather than as simply images that move, or as just a variant of theatre or discourse, and certainly as much more than as simply a further site for the instantiation of conceptual metaphors. From my first contact with the group and their studies of metaphor in film, I have been excited by the challenge they accept in taking film as their research focus and further by how their work contributes to the broader study of metaphor in human life. I find that, as our understanding of metaphor is enlarged through studying what happens with film, we are forced once more to confront the limitations imposed by seeing metaphor as a static figure of speech or thought. Metaphor in film refuses to be reduced to static figures as easily as text. Instead, a philosophical grounding for cinematic metaphor research is offered that begins from notions of expressive movement and movement-image. The studies of film in *Cinematic Metaphor* applying these notions empirically present cinematic metaphor as inherently dynamic, shifting and changing in the process of film-viewing.

https://doi.org/10.1515/9783110615036-002

In my Discourse Dynamics approach, I strive for a similar kind of understanding of metaphor in the dynamics of talk. This perspective was inspired by scholars such as Kittay (1987), Chafe (1994) and Linell (1998) who conceptualized discourse and conversation as *flow*. And it was inspired from outside linguistics by systems theory and its use of complexity theory and dynamic systems theory to account for the complex nature of ecological and biological systems (Larsen-Freeman and Cameron 2008). By viewing discourse in terms of complex dynamic systems, situated spoken interaction is understood as emerging from layered and interacting systems at various levels of scale, from the phonological to the historical. Film-making and film-viewing can be interpreted in terms of complex dynamic systems following similar arguments.

The inherent dynamics of film highlight, even more strongly than in the Discourse Dynamics approach, the inadequacy of considering 'metaphor' as grammatically nominal and (metaphorically) object. If our research context is written text, it may make sense to see metaphor as some kind of mental or visual/verbal object that is inserted into discourse and so can be extracted and described; there are, after all, words on a page or screen. However, when the context is film and we attend not to words, but to cinematic expressive movements, it becomes starkly obvious that 'metaphor' is not a discrete object and must instead be seen as process. Cinematic metaphor-making shifts and changes as the music plays, as the actors move, as the scene captured by the cameras changes, as the camera moves, as words are spoken, as the light intensifies and diminishes, as shadows are formed and disappear, and as all or some of this happens in combination. Cinematically, we see 'metaphorizing'.

This chapter reflects on what changes when we shift our perspective from metaphor to metaphorizing, from the discrete and static to the continuous, dynamic, from aggregations and sets to trajectories, from instances to flow.[1] I begin with consideration of how metaphorizing comes about in the flow of various kinds of creative activity and of film-viewing. The chapter then moves to consider implications of the metaphorizing/flow perspective for methodology and metaphor identification. An extract of conversation illustrates the evolution of a metaphorizing trajectory in the flow of talk. Finally, I turn to issues around the convention of reducing metaphor labels to the formulation 'A IS B', and offer suggestions for alternative formulations that better fit ideas of metaphorizing and flow.

---

[1] For such a shift in perspective with regard to audiovisual images see also Schmitt forthcoming/2019.

The varied nature of metaphorizing in the flow of talk and film

In the Discourse Dynamics approach, metaphorizing happens in a flow of interactional sense-making and 'languaging' (Swain 2009). However, by its very nature, this rich notion of discourse flow could never be as completely available to analysts as observable data. In my studies, I chose to work with recordings of talk in which we identified metaphorically-used words and phrases. These so-called 'verbal metaphors' can perhaps be better conceived of, not as instances of metaphor, but as traces of deeper processes of metaphorizing.

In attending mainly to the oral and aural, we fully recognized that many other aspects of situated social interaction were being neglected, including facial expressions, gaze, body movement and posture. And then there was always the rest of the interactional iceberg, invisible under the surface, including unspoken memories or resonances sparked by the talk, as well as participants' silent thoughts and inner speech.

Aspects of interaction cannot be studied separately and reassembled; metaphor in talk or in film cannot be studied as the sum of perceptual, physiological and psychological components. It is possible to break our data down and study the resulting parts, sometimes usefully, but, as for any complex dynamic system, these are not components that we can simply put back together again and then claim results about some larger type of 'metaphor'. The whole is greater than the sum of its parts. Rather, the experiential and the spoken are integral to each other in talk, and in film; meaning comes from each, and from their interplay. Metaphorizing is a process inside a process, a sub-system of the larger system. Metaphorizing of various types can occur, and in the following sub-section, I describe some of these.

Creative metaphorizing: from Vehicle to Topic

Creative artists of any kind – writers, painters, film-makers – are familiar with the sudden and unexpected arrival of metaphors, seemingly offering themselves 'out of the blue' for poetic purposes. And they do this in a reversal of the conventionally assumed process of metaphorizing. What appears are potential metaphor Vehicles in search of a Topic, rather than fully-fledged Topic~Vehicle combinations or Topics lacking Vehicles.[2]

---

[2] The terms 'Vehicle' and 'Topic' are capitalized here when they relate to metaphor. I prefer Vehicle to 'source domain' for data like talk (or film or image-making) that happens in real time.

I offer an example from my current, sleep-deprived, reality. An image from a television documentary – visual and aural, recalled and re-imagined – of a dry desert of unending blankness 'comes to mind', resonating with how it actually feels in the daytime after multiple sleepless nights with the baby. It's not that I was consciously working with the Topic of how it feels after sleepless nights and trying to find an appropriate Vehicle to describe it. Instead the desert Vehicle latched on to, or activated, a Topic relevant to me. If I had set out to make a metaphor, I might have thought long and hard about the sleepless nights, and never have found or created a desert image. The desert image spoke to my lived and felt experience, producing and enhancing meaning for me, in a kind of creative personal expressionism.

In this process of active, creative metaphorizing, the Vehicle does not so much transfer qualities from Vehicle to Topic, but does something more akin to awakening a metaphorical way of experiencing a Topic – to metaphorizing the Topic.

In this kind of metaphorizing, Topics sometimes take time to latch on to the proffered Vehicles. Several topics may try themselves against the potential of a Vehicle before settling down. And for a poet or artist concerned with producing a finished piece, there is work to do: the potential metaphor Vehicle must be noticed, grabbed hold of, and turned into something that contributes to the artwork. The artist performs a type of enhanced metaphorizing that extends and develops connections with potential topics to suit goals and materials. We may speak of this metaphorizing as poiesis.[3]

In an earlier article, I drew on descriptions by poets Seamus Heaney and Mark Doty of creative metaphorizing processes in action (Cameron 2011b). For Doty, a metaphorizing for the poem *Souls on Ice* began with noticing a supermarket display of fish laid out on ice: something about the shine of the mackerel and their eyes made a connection, however thin, to dead bodies, and to souls. The sight of the fish became a bridgehead for metaphor, a thin line sent first across the gap, to pull across a thicker rope, and then a making firm and the building of a safe passage for metaphor.

These examples of creative poietic metaphorizing are sparked by the concrete and visual, and not, at that first instant, the verbal or 'conceptual'. Afterwards comes an interplay of words and images and possibilities – the noticing,

---

At the timescale of seconds and minutes in talk, Vehicle terms are words or phrases. Not generalizing immediately to some larger source domain differentiates the Discourse Dynamics approach from Conceptual Metaphor Theory.

3 Poiesis: activity in which a person brings something into being that did not exist before.

verbalizing, connecting, and metaphor-shaping that is the poet's craft. The outcome of this poiesis is a poem, but it could also be a film or a painting.

Whether it be a poem or a film, after the intense attention and work of the makers, the outcome of poietic metaphorizing involves multiple metaphors, developing and interacting, twisting inside and around each other, connecting and separating, like a bird's nest built of interlacing metaphor twigs and cemented with mud; or like a Midas head of metaphor snakes, or a tangle of colored metaphor ribbons.

Poietic metaphorizing in film-viewing

Poietic metaphorizing does not, however, only belong to artists. In the approach of Müller, Kappelhoff and colleagues, film-viewing is also characterized as 'poiesis'. It is also dialogic. As in the Discourse Dynamics approach, cinematic metaphor theory goes beyond a simplistic code model of communication in which a producer encodes metaphors and meaning in films or talk, sending them to a receiver who decodes the same metaphors and meanings. The code model is replaced with a more subtle, interactional or dialogic model in which we are all participants in a continuing 'conversation' with ourselves and across time and culture. It is through this long conversation that we make meaning and sense of the world. There is no 'film' without interaction; the film exists in a kind of conversation with the viewer.

To imagine how processes of metaphorizing might happen in film-viewing, consider the 1936 film JEZEBEL (William Wyler, USA 1938), an analysis of which appears in Part 3 of the book *Cinematic Metaphor*. An early scene in the film features the appearance of the heroine Julie, played by Bette Davis, arriving late at a party in her honor on a large and difficult-to-control horse. She dismounts with a flourish and hands the reins to a small servant boy before flouncing into the house. Inside the house she walks straight into the party without changing her clothes and moves through the guests in their evening gowns in a tightly choreographed expressive movement, beautifully described in Section 3.1 of Müller and Kappelhoff (2018).

The woman's character is metaphorized through rhythms of movement and cessation of movement, i.e. movement of the main character through space and place and various types of camera/image movement: Julie riding the rearing horse and dismounting and holding it still by its bridle; Julie walking into the house, moving through the room, halted by her fiancé and his group; the camera zooming and stopping in a close-up shot; the camera panning the room and stopping.

The film viewer is exposed to these movement-images in all their complexity and potential. Some aspects of these may catch the attention and be the beginning of metaphorizing on the part of the viewer, consciously or not. What is noticed and attended to will depend to some extent on the viewers, who bring their long conversation with film and with life to the poiesis of viewing. Potential Vehicles may make connection with aspects of outside life as well as with Topics inside the film. The swirl of the actor's dress may echo the swirl of the horse's head; the determined woman making her way through a room of watching eyes until she is made small by being positioned next to a man may recall lived experience outside of the screening. Such fragments of connection can initiate creative metaphorizing on the part of the film viewer. As the film continues, some of these noticed connections may develop through further metaphorizing while others exist only in the moment or are discarded. Müller, Kappelhoff, and colleagues highlight through their delicate analyses how cinematic metaphorizing involves the entire film-viewing experience and beyond, and that, while it may be possible to pick out small-scale metaphors from individual scenes, this does not give an adequate understanding of the whole experience.

Intentional and potential metaphorizing

Sometimes the presence of metaphor in a film is intentional and explicitly declared as such by a director or screenwriter, as in this statement about the movie DOWNSIZING (Alexander Payne, USA 2017):

> Jim Taylor and I, when we started conceiving this screenplay 10 years ago, certainly had the idea to make on some level a political film – not literally or directly political, but something with a metaphor that would allow us to open the gates to certain hideous elements going on in current society. (Payne 2018)

Such explicitness happens less with talk and it is not usually possible to find evidence of active metaphorical meaning-making on the part of viewer. Only very rarely do participants in conversation offer evidence of active metaphor processing through explicit comments such as "… to coin a phrase …" or "… literally…" (Cameron and Deignan 2006).

In the absence of declared intention or explicit processing, we as researchers are left searching for latent potential metaphoricity. The next section considers methodological implications of adopting a metaphorizing perspective.

Metaphorizing and methodology

A metaphorizing and cinematic perspective shifts our attention as analysts away from single instances and towards trajectories, continuities, and evolving systems. It has been our practice to work from single instances out to larger systematic metaphors, but the shift in perspective suggests a shift in conceptualizing: what if the single instance of 'metaphor' is not the norm and starting point but instead is the limiting case of a metaphorizing flow? Each metaphorizing flow is a system with multiple potential connections, just as we saw with creative poietic metaphorizing. As a real world parallel, think of the London Underground, or some other transport system with frequent trains. Passengers think of trains in terms of their trajectory or route, not as a collection of one-off individual trains. The times of individual trains are usually unknown to passengers who wait for the next Jubilee Line train, not for the 09.34 train. We will hold this idea in mind as we consider how we have devised identification procedures.

In analyzing metaphor in spoken discourse, we search first for Vehicle terms. With metaphor characterized as seeing one thing in terms of another, a Vehicle term points to the 'another'. It contrasts with the ongoing discourse topic, yet connects and makes a kind of sense. In practice, this is a word-by-word and phrase-by-phrase search through the transcript,[4] spotting terms that contrast in some way and then checking them for potential metaphoricity (for full method, see Cameron et al. 2009, Cameron and Maslen 2010). Establishing the contrast (or tension) often requires drawing on some basic physical sense of Vehicle terms that would not be relevant in the discourse and topic context yet can be connected to bring extra meaning (Pragglejaz 2007).

In film, the equivalent to word/phrase level Vehicles would be expressive movements. Potentially metaphorical Vehicles can appear as strong contrasts with the ongoing flow of a film, but this seems to be unusual, particularly in the case of narratives where strong contrasts could be problematically disruptive. For example, the metaphorical dream sequence created by Salvador Dalí for SPELL-BOUND (Alfred Hitchcock, USA 1945) moves the film action to a clearly different time-space. It is supposedly a dream of one of the characters but is widely considered artistically unsuccessful. Another example of a strong and potentially metaphorical contrast would be a switch from color to monochrome, as occurs in THE CLOUDS OF SILS MARIA (Olivier Assayas, GER/FR/CH 2014); this striking move does mark a metaphorizing moment, but also requires incorporating it into

---

[4] I diverge from the Pragglejaz approach in requiring Vehicle terms to be words and phrases that are also units of meaning in the discourse rather than individual words.

the ongoing storyline – in this case, as an old film discovered by one the characters and inspiring his actions. Less obvious metaphorizing moves may be marked by some kind of multimodal cinematic 'tuning device': e.g., in JEZEBEL (William Wyler, USA 1938), the camera lingers on the difficult to control movements of the horse for an unusually long moment; as Gibbs relates in his chapter, images of parallel lines with accompanying music effects are repeated at crucial plot moments in SPELLBOUND, appearing on the tablecloth, on a bed cover, on snow (Gibbs 2018). Viewers' previous experience and cinematic expectations may be prompted by such signals to initiate metaphorizing, while analysts use them as additional evidence of potential metaphoricity.

Part of identifying a Vehicle term is to work out its connection to a Topic in the flow of conversation or film. Despite what may be suggested by simple 'A IS B' labels for metaphor, this is not unproblematic; specific Topic terms are in fact often more tricky to identify. Much more frequently, the Topic of the metaphor has to be re-constructed by the analyst, inferred from what is being said and has been said. In some cases, it is more productive to work with 'key discourse topics', finding a relatively small number across the discourse rather than local and specific Topic terms (e.g., Cameron 2011a). With a metaphorizing perspective, this problem turns around and becomes just what we would expect: that metaphor Topic is flow, not object.

Across a conversation or a series of conversations between the same participants, metaphor Vehicles may re-appear in similar or modified forms after their first appearance. Topics too might be modified by speakers. Extracted groups of semantically-linked verbal metaphor Vehicles used with the same or very similar Topic or key discourse topic are called 'systematic metaphors' (Cameron 2003, Maslen 2017). I first coined this term in 1997 when I was developing an analytic methodology for identifying metaphor in talk and found myself in need of an alternative theoretical concept from the then hegemonic idea of conceptual metaphor. I had started this first project intending to find 'conceptual metaphors in talk', or traces of them, but realized that such a phenomenon was, theoretically, a fallacy – conceptual metaphors are postulated thought systems, rather than individually 'held', abstracted by scholars from an imagined population on the basis of invented language data (Cameron 2008b, Deignan 2006). I decided that what was being identified in transcribed talk, often initially in the form of just a metaphor Vehicle, was more appropriately labelled 'verbal metaphor'. Systematic metaphors are then collections of connected verbal metaphors across discourse. Furthermore, because each instance of a verbal metaphor Vehicle occurs at a specific time point in the talk, systematic metaphors are also trajectories of connected verbal metaphors across discourse. Here the two perspectives coincide: metaphorizing trajectories running through the flow of talk and occasionally becoming visible/systematic metaphors as collections of related verbal metaphors.

In his chapter, Raymond W. Gibbs (this volume) describes such a metaphorizing trajectory running through the film SPELLBOUND. Out of the flow of the film certain expressive movements stand out to viewer/analyst as traces of a metaphorizing process on the part of the film-maker and potential metaphorizing on the part of the film viewer.

We can zoom out further in our search for metaphorizing trajectories and consider series of conversations and films over timescales of months and years. At these zoomed-out levels, the Discourse Dynamics approach accounts for the stabilizing of certain metaphors as 'metaphoremes' and idioms (Cameron and Deignan 2006, Deignan 2017). Local one-off verbal metaphors reflect emerging metaphorizing trajectories that connect into more communal discourse levels through emergence and self-organizing complex dynamic systems; as grammatical, lexical, phonological features stabilize over time, the trajectory collapses into a limited set of forms and crystallize into idioms. More relevant for film perhaps, Larsen-Freeman and Cameron show how genres can emerge from dynamic processes of languaging over time (Larsen-Freeman and Cameron 2008).

Metaphorizing and the labelling issue

I have for many years been uncomfortable with the apparently unquestioned formulation of metaphors with 'A IS B' labels, and am glad of this opportunity to discuss some of the issues that are rendered even more visible when we attend to cinematic metaphorizing as expressive movement.

I suggest that not only does it not attend sufficiently to differing research goals to reduce all types of metaphoricity to an A is B formulation, but it is also theoretically inadequate. Of course, these reductive labels are intended to work as shorthand, mnemonic, pointers to what a metaphor does and means. But we know as linguists that naming and labelling is never innocent. How we name relates to how we classify, which is in itself a theoretical move, and reflects and influences how we think about what is labelled.

The problems

The first issue relates to the form of the label: the grammar of 'A IS B', with its copular verb IS, insists on the identity of the entity lexicalized by the subject noun phrase A with its noun phrase complement B. The first inadequacy lies in the assumption of identity: there is no identity in the metaphorizing of a Topic by a Vehicle, rather there is connecting across difference. The second inadequacy arises from forcing Topics and Vehicles into the form of nouns or noun phrases; for example, in my analyses of metaphorizing in conversation, I found that Vehicle terms were more likely to be verbs as nouns (Cameron 2003, 2008a) and reformulating Vehicle verbs into noun form risked losing something important about the data. Deignan's work (e.g., 2006) has long shown that metaphoricity is not grammatically-neutral.

The particular 'A IS B' form seems to derive from literary examples of textual metaphor, such as *Juliet is the sun*. And yet such formulations are extremely rare, even in literature – I suspect that the difficulty of finding examples accounts for the repeated appearance of the same examples in theoretical texts over decades. Constructed examples have a tendency to sound weird or wildly over-generalizing: consider *billboards are warts on the landscape* or LOVE IS WAR (Lakoff and Johnson 1980).

A second issue is that often, especially in real-world data, there is simply no A to be identified – we cannot explicitly describe in a simple noun phrase what is being metaphorized as topic in talk or in film. The nature of creative poietic metaphorizing described earlier in the chapter accounts for why this might be so. Firstly, the Vehicle arrives with no more than a feeling for a possible Topic. Then the poet or film-maker can play with the ambiguities of Vehicle – Topic connection during poiesis. The Topic may not need to be present as more than a hint at this stage, taking on sharper focus as the film or discourse event proceeds.

Furthermore, the dynamic interactions of metaphorizing immediately shift what might initially have been being thought about – once I've metaphorized the feeling of sleepless nights as desert blankness, that sleep-deprived feeling no longer exists for me without traces of the desert image.

A third set of problems arises with the minimal formulation of 'A IS B' as we move from one-off metaphors to something more systematic. Once we collect more than one instance of a Vehicle in relation to a given Topic, we are faced with the non-trivial problem of choosing which term to put in the B slot.

Do we go to the highest levels of generality or abstraction, e.g., TIME IS SPACE? Or do we go for more concrete/specific terms, e.g., combining *zombie state, fog, desert* into something like SLEEPLESSNESS IS AN EXTERNALLY BLANKED MIND?

How important is it to respect the limits of metaphor? Only certain aspects of a Vehicle semantic field are drawn on in relation to a given Topic field. Corpus evidence shows that this is an important aspect of metaphor more widely. Generalizing the B term beyond this limit may lead to drawing over-generalized conclusions from studies.

By turning from metaphor to metaphorizing, some alternatives to the 'A IS B' formulation can be offered. Below I discuss three of these, beginning with the reversal suggested by the poiesis of creative metaphorizing.

An alternative formulation for metaphorizing

A first step concerns the ordering of 'A IS B', which implies a separately existing Topic (A) modified by the Vehicle (B). As we saw above, creative poietic metaphorizing involves a Vehicle arriving and prompting a Topic, in a reversal:

B metaphorizes A

The second step is to replace the verb with a more complex symbol, the tilde ~ chosen for its theoretical necessity and its poetic possibilities.

B~A

The tilde sign ~ is appropriated to indicate the indefinable, non-finalizable, back and forth connection between two disparate notions or entities that, up to now, we have called Vehicle and Topic. The metaphor emerges from the connecting of the two, coming out of their metaphorizing relationship: M comes from V~T.

Using the tilde in such a way has its roots in mathematics, where it connects two expressions in a binary relation. Two functions connected with a tilde are, at their limit, equivalent. In geometry, the tilde expresses congruence. In logic, it signals negation: ~P is 'not P', all that is not P; the complement of P rather than its opposite. In physics and astronomy, it indicates that two expressions are of the same order of magnitude. Far away from mathematics, medieval scribes used tilde signs in manuscripts to mark an omission of letters, but only letters so obvious that the reader could supply what was missing and the scribe could save a little vellum and ink.

Appropriating the tilde ~ to replace the IS in the formulation 'A IS B' thus increases adequacy because it symbolizes not only equivalence, but also the difference between V and T required for metaphoricity, and the unfinalizability of the connecting back and forth between them.

Adding in the step of reversing the linear sequence of A and B in order to better reflect the direction of metaphorizing, we end up with the formulation:

V ~ T → M_{ing} (where M_{ing} stands for metaphorizing)

Returning to the example of baby-driven sleep deprivation, my metaphorizing might be formulated as:

M_{ing} *a dry desert of unending blankness ~ how the sleepless nights feel*

Alternative formulations for systematic metaphor as metaphorizing trajectory

With the tilde in hand as a symbol for connecting and metaphorizing, let's now return to the twisting nests of metaphorizing connections, the Medusa's hair – that build up across the longer timescales of one or more conversations or films, and the theoretical and methodological issues around how these are formulated.

How then to formulate a descriptive label for a systematic metaphor as a trajectory of connected metaphorizing across the flow of a specific discourse event or longer timescale? To answer this question, it may help to unpack the nature of systematic metaphorizing with a new example.

Instead of the conceptual metaphor theoretic notion of pre-existing, highly generalized, conceptual metaphors, which wait, object-like, to be brought out of some mental cupboard to be used, we have a dialogical constructing, compiling process in which an initial Vehicle appears, is offered for metaphorizing, and initiates a trajectory of further Vehicles that relate to the first through *ad hoc*, in the moment, processes such as elaboration, contrast and relexicalization (Cameron 2008b).

We can watch this happening in the following extracts from a life coaching session between the author and a coach, here called A.[5] A skype session, audio only, took place in July 2013, was recorded, and later transcribed into approximate intonation units, omitting pauses and hesitations.

The discourse topic had been agreed upon by the participants and is recapitulated by the coach in line 1 as *being fully present*. The feeling of *being present* is first metaphorized through contrast: *not fizzing around*, then reversed and made more specific: *a big sandy beach*. The *beach* metaphor then evolves through a trajectory of linked Vehicles. Vehicle terms are underlined.

    1   A: Your intention is to be more <u>in</u> the present.
                  so what would that <u>feel</u> like?
                  …
        LC: I'm <u>not fizzing around</u>.
        A: What are you?
    5 LC: I'm <u>calm</u>, <u>like a big sandy beach</u>.
                  …
                  the beach is quite a good analogy isn't it?
                  because

---

[5] Some stretches of talk are omitted because of space constraints; these are indicated by three dots …

	I love walking over rocks but you really have to be there in
	the moment to jump from one rock to the next
10	and not to break your ankle or something,
	but if it's a big flat sandy beach
	you don't have to think about what you're walking.
	And I think I'd just like to be <u>on a big flat sandy beach</u> for a bit
	'cos it <u>feels</u> like I'm <u>jumping from one rock to the next</u> all the
	time.
15	And while I love doing that
	because it makes me <u>feel</u> agile,
	it's quite exhausting really
	...
	I'm <u>moving across it</u>
	<u>but without the effort.</u>
20	I'm <u>not having to attend to</u>
	<u>where I put my feet</u>
	...
	I can <u>see where I'm going</u>
	I can <u>enjoy looking at the sea instead of looking at my feet.</u>
	I can <u>see the horizon</u>
25	and the other people that are there
	and
	So it's not
	<u>a blind meandering</u>
	it's just <u>not having to attend to</u>
30	<u>exactly every step</u>

Coaching conversations are particularly likely to encourage intensive elaboration of metaphor as part of their exploration of assumptions and possibilities, and further metaphorized development of the ideas continued after this extract. Later in the conversation, in another move characteristic of coaching, A offered a summarizing question to use a tool for future reflection on life choices and activities: *Where's the beach in this?* The metaphor Vehicle *the beach* has, at this point, come to work metonymically to represent that stabilized systematic metaphor that emerged through the extended metaphorizing.

The extract displays various features of a metaphorizing phenomenon that in earlier work I called 'metaphor shifting' (Cameron 2008b). Both Vehicle and, to a lesser extent, Topic, shift and change, creating the trajectory of the systematic metaphor. The dynamics of cinematic metaphor show similar processes;

systematic cinematic metaphorizing trajectories emerge through a sequence of shifts that can be multi-modal and intricately interwoven (Müller and Kappelhoff 2018).

The extract provides examples of robust features of metaphor shifting:

(1) *An often under-specified Topic*
Here it shifts between coach and client until it settles for a while in the second half of the extract:

how it feels *to be more present* (1–2)
→ the client herself: *I'm not...; ...you; I'm...* (3–5)
→ what the client is doing that makes her feel exhausted: *it's* (17)
→ the feeling of not being exhausted and being more present: (18–29)
→ something in the client's life: *it's* (26–27)

(2) *A slippery relation between Topic and Vehicle*
The client's elaboration (6–12) of how it actually feels to walk on rocks and sand takes the metaphorizing Vehicle of *a beach* and literalizes it. Although she speaks in these lines of non-metaphorical beach experiences, the potential metaphorizing effect of *the beach* continues since both coach and client have so recently used it as metaphor. In line 13, *to be on a big flat sandy beach* seems to mark a return to metaphorizing but retains a sense of the literal beach of previous lines.[6]

(3) *Blurred Vehicle boundaries*
This point relates closely to (2) above, in which Topic and Vehicle overlap. Although one or more lexical items clearly mark Vehicle talk, immediately surrounding items may less clearly be part of the Vehicle. For example, *see the horizon* (24) seems to be metaphorical, whereas *the other people that are there* is more doubtful. The ambiguity of articles and pronouns add to Vehicle blurring.[7]

(4) *Vehicle shifting*

(4.1) Vehicle repetition: The conversation included several occurrences of *big flat sandy beach* and close variants. Although we may call these 'repetitions', it is important to note that a dynamic approach denies the possibility of repetition; each use changes the system and so each use is unique.

(4.2) Vehicle explication: *moving across it → attend to where I put my feet, see where I'm going* etc. (18–24)

---

[6] And it seems more than coincidence that I now have a house close to just such a beach and walk on it regularly.
[7] Vehicle boundary blurring only causes problems for counting Vehicles if single words are to be counted.

(4.3) Vehicle contrast: on a big flat sandy beach → jumping from one rock to the next (13–14)

(5) *Second order metaphorizing*
A Vehicle can itself be metaphorized: *not a blind meandering* (27) metaphorizes the earlier Vehicles *moving across* (18) and *a big flat sandy beach* (13).

Finding a short formulation to act as a label for all the metaphorizing in the extract needs to bear these features in mind. We can also notice the limits of the metaphorizing. Many aspects of walking on a sandy beach are not evoked by speakers: for example, exposure to cold winds, the possibility of taking off socks and shoes to paddle, the noise of birds, the distressing presence of plastic waste. Any labelling should respect these limits.

The example demonstrates that, with a systematic metaphor, even more so than with a one-off instance of metaphorizing, we are dealing with a trajectory of shifting, change, and adaptation that resists the non-dynamic nature of an 'A IS B' label. Labelling cinematic metaphor in film faces similar problems. In the hope that discussing this issue will help it find a place on the research agenda of contemporary metaphor scholars, I offer the following suggestions and questions for further development.

Back in 1997, I adopted the '*A IS B*' form for systematic metaphor, insisting on it being formatted in italics to signal that it was extracted from real world data and not assumed to be a pre-existing conceptual metaphor. I also established the principles that the systematic Vehicle should be (a) not be at a higher level of generality or abstraction than is required to include all Vehicle items, and (b) formulated where possible out of actual lexical items used by participants. In an attempt to mitigate the dangers of data reduction, I also insisted on the methodological principle that any descriptive label remains connected to the data from which it is derived, which, in practice, means that transcriptions are available to be referred to at all times.

While suggesting V~T to replace 'A IS B', I would retain these principles. We might then describe the metaphorizing trajectory, or systematic metaphor, in the coaching conversation with a short descriptive summary in which participles are employed to reflect the mostly verb Vehicles in the talk:

M_{ing}

the calm experience of walking on a big flat sandy beach and being able to look up and see all around ~ *the desired feeling of being fully present in everyday life*

Alternative formulations for historically systematic metaphor as metaphorizing trajectory

The level of granularity, abstraction or semantic generality most appropriate for the set of Vehicle terms is rarely obvious, even across one film or conversation. When we widen our scope and consider metaphorizing processes on longer timescales – a book, a film, a lifetime, cultural movements, historical – the issue only deepens. In a study of conciliation conversations between the same two people over a period of ten years (Cameron 2007, 2011a), I explored a further possibility for describing a set of connected systematic metaphors. To enable greater detail, I carefully composed what we might call a 'metaphorizing narrative' that drew on their most frequent Vehicles while at the same time respecting the limits of their metaphors.

Jo Berry's father was killed by a bomb placed in a Brighton hotel by Patrick Magee in 1984. They first met in 2000 and continue to meet and to talk in public events about their process of conciliation. Across the multiple datasets made available to me, I identified four major groupings of metaphor Vehicles used systematically in talks around the topic of CONCILIATION and labelled them as:

– JOURNEYS
– CONNECTION
– SEEING MORE CLEARLY
– LISTENING TO A STORY

In place of 'A IS B' labels such as CONCILIATION IS A JOURNEY, the metaphorizing narrative offers a deeper picture of how the four systematic metaphor trajectories overlap, interlace, and evolve over the course of the participants' long-term interaction.

The metaphorizing narrative constructed from participants' use of these systematic metaphors:

> [...] is an interpretive synthesis constructed by the researcher from the results of the analysis that attempts to remain as close as possible to the words of the participants. The coherence of the scenario is partial, with incompleteness and some incoherences. It is negotiated, sometimes contested, and interim, presenting a fairly stable scenario that has emerged from the dynamics of the talk covered in this study, but a temporary stabilization that may change through further conversations, actions or events.

> After the bombing, Jo and Pat complete separate journeys, long and on foot, until they meet face-to-face and try to connect across the gap between their experiences. Jo's journey has the aim of understanding the roots of violence and is a long, uphill journey on foot, sometimes following the path of journeys made by the bombers, sometimes stopping to meet other victims. The journey out of grief becomes a healing process. Pat does not talk much about his life up between the bombing and the meeting, but speaks of an earlier journey when, as a young man, he joined the IRA and agreed to use violence.
>
> When Jo and Pat meet and sit down to talk to each other, it is, for both and in different ways, a momentous point in their journeys. It is not, however, where the journeys end, rather it is a new starting point. For Pat, meeting Jo is a confrontation with an unavoidable obstacle, the consequences of his actions. He has to face this and cannot walk away from it. He can however come through this dark phase of his journey.
>
> When Jo and Pat meet, they need to open channels of communication between them. For Jo, and then also for Pat, connection comes through being open, which may require the breaking down of barriers. Jo wants to build bridges to cross the gap between them. Through careful listening to the story that the Other tells, each comes to know and understand the Other better – they can see the Other more clearly and more completely.

(Cameron 2007, 206, frame around parts of the text in the original)

The 'A IS B' formulation may be appropriate for studies under the umbrella of conceptual metaphor theory; they come with a set of theoretical assumptions. The shift in perspective to metaphorizing and flow prompted by cinematic metaphor has generated alternatives for dynamic situations: reversal and the use of the tilde in describing metaphorizing instances, $V{\sim}T \to M_{ing}$; short descriptive summaries of metaphorizing trajectories; the metaphorizing narrative to describe multiple interwoven trajectories.

Conclusion

Adopting a cinematic perspective has taken us further down the road of understanding metaphor as a kind of living organism that emerges, grows, flourishes and eventually declines. This has been explored by shifting how we can think about metaphor in terms of metaphorizing processes in the flow of speech and film-viewing. Rather than seeing verbal metaphors as Topics modified by Vehicles, we have noted how creative artists often experience a reversal of this process when a concrete and visual Vehicle offers itself for metaphorizing. This reversal took us into finding alternatives formulations of metaphor that may be more adequate to describe dynamic systems and processes.

I hope to have demonstrated how understandings from cinematic metaphor, refracted back into the full range of metaphor studies, have the potential to open up rich new perspectives. The journey has just begun.

Audiovisual sources

DOWNSIZING, Dir. Alexander Payne, Paramount Pictures, USA 2017.
JEZEBEL, Dir. William Wyler, Warner Bros., USA 1938.
SPELLBOUND, Dir. Alfred Hitchcock, Selznick International Pictures, USA 1945.
THE CLOUDS OF SILS MARIA, Dir. Olivier Assayas, CG Cinéma GER/FR/CH 2014.

Bibliography

Cameron, Lynne. 2003. *Metaphor in Educational Discourse, Advances in Applied Linguistics*. London: Continuum.

Cameron, Lynne. 2007. "Patterns of Metaphor Use in Reconciliation Talk." *Discourse & Society* 18 (2): 197–222.

Cameron, Lynne. 2008a. "Metaphor and Talk." In *The Cambridge Handbook of Metaphor and Thought*, edited by Raymond W. Jr. Gibbs, 197–211. Cambridge: Cambridge University Press.

Cameron, Lynne. 2008b. "Metaphor Shifting in Discourse." In *Confronting Metaphor in Use. An Applied Linguistic Approach*, edited by Maria Sophia Zanotto, Lynne Cameron, and Maria Cavalcanti, 197–211. Amsterdam: John Benjamins.

Cameron, Lynne. 2011a. *Metaphor and Reconciliation. The Discourse Dynamics of Empathy in Post-Conflict Conversations*. New York, NY: Routledge.

Cameron, Lynne. 2011b. "Metaphor in Prosaic and Poetic Creativity." In *Language and Creativity. The State of the Art*, edited by Joan Swann, Robert Pope, and Ronald Carter, 66–82. London: Palgrave Macmillan.

Cameron, Lynne, and Alice Deignan. 2006. "The Emergence of Metaphor in Discourse." *Applied Linguistics* 27 (4): 671–690.

Cameron, Lynne, and Robert Maslen, eds. 2010. *Metaphor Analysis. Research Practice in Applied Linguistics*. London: Equinox.

Cameron, Lynne, Robert Maslen, Zazie Todd, John Maule, Peter Stratton, and Neil Stanley. 2009. "The Discourse Dynamics Approach to Metaphor and Metaphor-Led Discourse Analysis." *Metaphor & Symbol* 24: 1–27.

Chafe, Wallace. 1994. *Discourse, Consciousness, and Time. The Flow and Displacement of Conscious Experience in Speaking and Writing*. Chicago, IL: University of Chicago Press.
Deignan, Alice. 2006. *Metaphor in Corpus Linguistics*. Amsterdam: John Benjamins.
Deignan, Alice. 2017. "Mappings and Narrative in Figurative Communication." In *Metaphor. Embodied Cognition and Discourse*, edited by Beate Hampe, 200–219. Cambridge: Cambridge University Press.
Gibbs, Raymond W. Jr. 2018. "Our Metaphorical Experiences of Film." In *Cinematic Metaphor in Perspective. Reflections on a Transdisciplinary Framework*, edited by Sarah Greifenstein, Dorothea Horst, Thomas Scherer, Christina Schmitt, Hermann Kappelhoff, and Cornelia Müller, 120–140. Berlin/Boston, MA: Walter de Gruyter.
Kittay, Eva Feder. 1987. *Metaphor. Its Cognitive Force and Linguistic Structure*. Oxford: Clarendon Press.
Lakoff, George, and Mark Johnson. 1980. *Metaphors We Live By*. Chicago, IL: University of Chicago Press.
Larsen-Freeman, Diane, and Lynne Cameron. 2008. *Complex Systems and Applied Linguistics*. Oxford: Oxford University Press.
Linell, Per. 1998. *Approaching Dialogue. Talk, Interaction and Contexts in Dialogical Perspectives*. Amsterdam: John Benjamins.
Maslen, Robert. 2017. "Finding Systematic Metaphors." In *The Routledge Handbook of Metaphor and Language*, edited by Elena Semino and Zsofia Demjén, 88–101. Abingdon: Routledge.
Müller, Cornelia, and Hermann Kappelhoff. 2018. *Cinematic Metaphor. Experience – Affectivity – Temporality*. In collaboration with Sarah Greifenstein, Dorothea Horst, Thomas Scherer, and Christina Schmitt. Berlin/Boston, MA: Walter de Gruyter.
Payne, Alexander. 2018 (January 7). Alexander Payne on Downsizing: 'The film isn't a major statement – it's a metaphor'. *The Guardian*. https://www.theguardian.com/film/2018/jan/07/alexander-payne-downsizing-interview-matt-damon. Accessed 16 February 2018.
Pragglejaz. 2007. "MIP: A Method for Identifying Metaphorically Used Words In Discourse." *Metaphor & Symbol* 22 (1): 1–40.
Schmitt, Christina. forthcoming/2019. *Wahrnehmen, fühlen, verstehen. Metaphorisieren und audiovisuelle Bilder*. Berlin/Boston, MA: Walter de Gruyter.
Swain, Merrill. 2009. "Languaging, Agency and Collaboration in Advanced Second Language Proficiency." In *Advanced Language Learning. The Contribution of Halliday and Vygotsky*, edited by Heidi Byrnes, 95–108. London: AC Black.

Michael Wedel
Murnau and Metaphor: From Cinematic Expressionism to Cinematic Expressive Movements

At least since the publication of Michael Henry's *Le cinéma expressioniste allemande. Un langage métaphorique* (1971), Weimar art cinema, and German expressionist film in particular, has figured in film theory and film historiography as one of the key examples of a 'metaphorical' film style. A qualification that has acquired paradigmatic status, this notion has been based on the formal properties of such canonical films as DAS CABINET DES DR. CALIGARI (Robert Wiene, GER 1920) and METROPOLIS (Fritz Lang, GER 1927): the symbolic stylization of the sets, the complex organization of space, and the deviation from principles of classical narration and continuity editing have been understood as producing an allegorical mode of cinematic representation and storytelling marked by the frequent use of subjective flashbacks, dream sequences, and multiple narrative framings.

Trevor Whittock, in his book *Metaphor and Film*, argues along similar lines when he asserts: "Metaphors of the distortion type based on mise-en-scène range from the expressive sets of Robert Wiene's THE CABINET OF DR. CALIGARI [...] to the mood lighting effects of film noir" (Whittock 1990, 64). With explicit reference to Henry, Thomas Elsaesser characterizes expressionist film as an "'excessively' metaphoric textual system, where the institution itself, i.e., the filmmaker, the audience, the screen appear as a *mise-en-abyme* and mirror images of each other, in infinite regress" (Elsaesser 2000, 75–76). In Elsaesser's revisionist account of Weimar cinema, the implicit metaphorical logic of cinematic expressionism serves not only as the methodological starting point, but also as a central template across which all kinds of films from the Weimar period – popular genre films as much as works aspiring to the ranks of art – can be re-read as belonging to a cultural formation resting on the unsteady grounds of allegorical "picture puzzles" that "refuse to be tied down to a single meaning" (Elsaesser 2000, 4).

Shadows and shadowings: Metaphor/metonymy in film theory

Along with Soviet montage cinema of the 1920s (Ropars-Wuilleumier 1978), French surrealist films of the 1920s and early 1930s (Williams 1976, 1981a, b, 53–105), or Hollywood's films noir of the 1940s and 1950s (Kaplan 1998, Naremore 2008, 18–37) – the latter often considered as a continuation of the stylistic parameters of cinematic expressionism – Weimar cinema has come to stand as another *locus classicus* for conceptualizing and historicizing forms of cinematic metaphoricity. In the course of identifying these paradigmatic cases, the film theoretical appropriation of the concept of metaphor and the concomitant introduction of linguistic tropes and forms of literary figurativity into the field of film studies has been guided by Roman Jakobson's basic distinction between metaphor and metonymy and Christian Metz's extensive elaboration on this distinction in *Psychoanalysis and Cinema. The Imaginary Signifier* (Metz 1982).

In his essay "Two Aspects of Language and Two Types of Aphasic Disturbances", Jakobson (1956) briefly addressed the question of how the metaphor/metonymy distinction could be related to the principal formal elements of film. Whereas he describes the close-up as a form based on the principle of synecdoche and film editing as a metonymical operation, he suggests that 'superimposed dissolves' should be understood as 'filmic similes' and thus cinematic equivalents of metaphorical processes (Jakobson 1971 [1956], 86, 92).

Metz took up Jakobson's designations and criticized them for the simple one-to-one relationships they set up. Neither could "'superimposed dissolves' be attributed en bloc to the metaphorical principle" nor is "[e]diting, in itself, [...] metonymical: it is syntagmatic" (Metz 1982, 194). Metz went on to show that distinctions between metonymy and metaphor cannot be made on the basis of formal film elements alone but should instead take into account the various levels on which similarity and contiguity operate in concrete configurations between the diegetic and the extra-diegetic, the referential and the discursive. As a consequence, in their actual distribution within a given film or group of films, metonymical and metaphorical operations rarely appear in pure forms but rather in figurations of intersection and mutual implication (Metz 1982, 200).

A case in point for Metz is expressionist cinema's play with shadows. The particular film he mentions, without discussing it in any detail, is Arthur Robison's SCHATTEN (WARNING SHADOWS, GER 1923). On the one hand, as Metz points out, shadows – bound as they are to the contiguity of a body or object by which they are cast – are "metonymic by definition"; on the other hand, they are "impure" metonymies insofar as they also establish a comparative relationship of similarity and transference (Metz 1982, 206). As such, one can infer from Metz's brief reference to the use of shadows in expressionist film (and in horror cinema) that this second dimension to which he alludes is not reducible to a purely mimetic relationship but is instead dynamic, open to ambiguity and disruption of the semantic field. It can thus be understood as carrying the potential for metaphorical shifts in meaning.

The dream sequence in SCHLOSS VOGELÖD as figurative event

Even though Metz characterizes metaphor and metonymy as dynamic figures, overlapping and intersecting in changing patterns of dominance, his main interest is to provide a general classification for how the economy of cinematic discourse is structured by processes of selection and ordering (understood with reference to Freud and Lacan in analogy to the workings of the unconscious and the dream with its three levels of condensation, displacement, and secondarization). As Dudley Andrew has observed, the model Metz provides for the analysis of cinematic figuration is not itself dynamic, but rather static in its structuralist view of film as a medium that generates meaning through narrative and that privileges metonymy (Andrew 1984, 167): "All figuration for him is merely displaced narration" (Andrew 1984, 170). From a Metzian perspective, metaphorical figurations in film, such as the excessive use of shadows in expressionist film, function as occasional irritations and calculated interruptions in the discursive and narrative economy of filmic signification, as overdetermined forms of expressivity shaped by the presence of 'unconscious' psychic energies.

A closer look at another example from the early Weimar period reveals the benefits but also the limits of such a view on the function of metaphor in film. Interpreted along the same lines as Metz's argument, the dream sequence in Friedrich Wilhelm Murnau's SCHLOSS VOGELÖD (GER 1921) appears as a radical discursive intervention in and stylistic deviation from what otherwise seems to be a 'realist' *Kammerspielfilm* (chamber play film) painstakingly observing the rules of the unity of time, place, and narrative.

The film's action takes place over three days at a country manor where a group of aristocrats have assembled for the annual autumn hunt. They are guests of the Lord of the Castle Vogelschrey and his wife Centa. Due to bad weather, the hunt is repeatedly postponed. After the unsolicited appearance of Count Oetsch, an outcast of the local aristocracy ever since coming under suspicion for killing his own brother out of greed, the unresolved murder case becomes the main topic of the conversation among the group as they wait for the weather to change.[1] All the more so, since the victim's widow, Baroness Safferstädt, is expected to arrive at the mansion soon with her new husband to join the hunting party. Also expected at the manor is Father Faramund from Rome, a relative of the murder

---

[1] Much of the film's action takes place while the guests at the manor are waiting for the weather to change. Steve Choe (2014, 62–74) has taken this narrative set-up as the basis for reading SCHLOSS VOGELÖD as an allegory of melancholy.

victim. When the Baroness learns that Father Faramund is coming, she decides to confess to him that it was her current husband who killed her first one after he misunderstood her intentions. As the film develops in a slow succession of doublings and reversals and of absences and presences, it becomes clear that Count Oetsch appears on the scene disguised as Father Faramund in order to find out the truth from the Baroness and restore his honor. After the truth has come to light – in a number of slow-paced scenes, intensifying the atmosphere of doom and guilt rather than rushing to a dramatic climax –, the film takes a tragic turn, as was characteristic of the German *Kammerspielfilm* of the early 1920s. The husband of the Baroness commits suicide, while the Baroness, widowed for the second time, faces a life wrecked twice.

SCHLOSS VOGELÖD follows the main spatial logic of the *Kammerspiel* genre insofar as it presents the deterioration of a community as motivated by an outside intrusion of something alien – in this case the double appearance of the outcast Count Oetsch/Father Faramund. In this respect, the film's dream sequence (one of two in the film) may indeed appear as a 'metaphor of distortion' in Whittock's sense and, along the Metzian paradigm, as an overdetermined expressive (and expressionist) figuration of the film's main poetic principle and generic formula, filtered through the unconscious fantasy of one of its characters – in this case one of the invited guests at the castle, tellingly introduced in the film's opening credits as "the anxious gentleman" ("Ängstlicher Herr").

The sequence (Figure 1) is explicitly announced as a dream by an intertitle ("Dreams" [Träume]) and thus clearly marked as not belonging to the world of 'objective' reality represented in the film. A first shot, initiated by a widening iris mask, shows the character asleep in bed (the reality status of this image is somewhat uncertain: does it belong to 'objective' reality showing the character dreaming, or are we already within the dream reality in which the character dreams of himself sleeping?). In the next shot a monstrous, clawed hand appears outside the bedroom window. From this second medium shot, the film then cuts to a long shot, integrating the two previous partial views: the window has now been pushed open and the hand extends on a periscope-like outstretched arm across the room to grasp 'the anxious gentleman' who wakes up in shock. The act of grasping itself is detailed in a medium close-up and divided into two phases: first, the shadow of the hand slowly approaching and finally falling on the body of 'the anxious gentleman', then the hand itself dragging the man out of his bed and off-screen right. The dream sequence's final shot returns to the previous central position: a distanced view of the room with the now-empty bed on the left and the window through which we see the character disappearing under the steady grip of the monstrous hand on the right. The next shot, filmed from a similar but not identical camera position and starting with a widening iris mask (like the shot

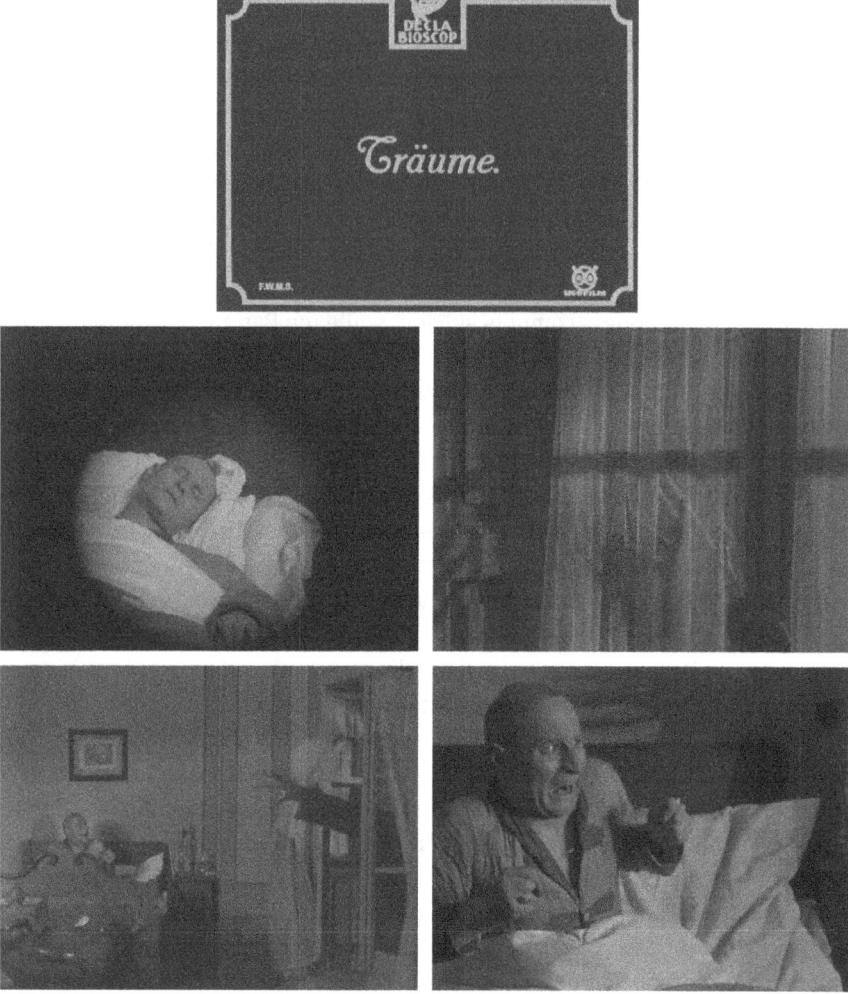

Figure 1: Dream sequence in SCHLOSS VOGELÖD.

at the beginning of the sequence), shows 'the anxious gentleman' back in bed, waking up and looking confused toward the direction of the window, which is now kept off-screen through framing.

A more traditional reading of the metaphorical operations at work in this sequence would consider it as a subjective representation of distorted reality based on the analogy of the dream work's processes of condensation and transference. In tune with what has been argued about the stylized reality of the frame narrative in DAS CABINET DES DR. CALIGARI (cf. Kracauer 1947, 61–76,

Budd 1990, 36–51, Scheunemann 2003), the recourse to expressionist set- and prop-design, high contrast lighting, and the use of cast shadows would be explained within this interpretive scenario as a moment of visual excess anchored in a character's (pathological) subjective fantasy. It is therefore not coincidental that the dream sequence from SCHLOSS VOGELÖD has been compared with the staging of the first murder scene in DAS CABINET DES DR. CALIGARI (Sadowski 2018, 119).

But considering the function of metaphors in the context of narrative cinema as isolated instances of stylistic excess, or as disruptive avantgarde moments of deviation from an otherwise consistently ordered fictional world, excludes a number of crucial theoretical implications and analytical insights. It was, again, Dudley Andrew who voiced his discontent with the way figuration, and especially metaphor, is conceptualized within film studies, making a claim for a radical reversal in our thinking about metaphor and metonymy:

> The metaphor demands close description since by definition no rule or convention can determine or locate its utility and scope. As it is elaborated in detail it becomes a model for the redescription of reality as such. Only the manifold of experience can determine the extent of metaphor's power [...] For structuralism will not recognize the event of cinematic discourse. It will always and only provide a description of the system which is put into use in the event. If [...] the system was born and exists only as a residue of such events of figuration, then we need a broader vision of the creation of meaning in films. (Andrew 1984, 169–170)

It seems to me that the model of cinematic metaphor proposed by Cornelia Müller, Hermann Kappelhoff, and colleagues (2018) allows for such a broader, experience-based theoretical perspective. As Müller and Kappelhoff put it:

> only when metaphoricity is grounded in this media-specific perceptual experience, can we speak of cinematic metaphors. Cinematic metaphors emerge in a process of affective perception of cinematic expressive movements. They are emergent, dynamic, temporally structured and grounded in the rhythms, intensities and other affective qualities of cinematic expressivity. (Müller and Kappelhoff 2018, 179)

By introducing the heuristic category of *cinematic expressive movements* as "a form of cinematic composition that modulates affective experiences of film viewers" (Müller and Kappelhoff 2018, 129) and thus offers access to the overall compositional *gestalt* which shapes the processes from which metaphorical meaning emerges in the temporal unfolding of a film, the model of cinematic metaphor provides the analytical instruments for the close description that Andrew deems necessary to conceive of metaphor "not as a verbal substitution but as a process resulting in the redescription of a semantic field" and for the concept to become "useful to film theory" (Andrew 1984, 167) at all.

Worlds, atmospheres, and the poetics of affect

In contrast to structuralist film theory which sees metaphorical constructions as punctual occurrences within an otherwise metonymically stitched together diegetic universe, Müller and Kappelhoff consider the process of metaphorization as constitutive for creating a cinematic world, key to what Andrew (1984: 169) calls the filmic "redescription of reality":

> [...] what makes up a cinematic metaphor is that it unfolds over the course of the film in ever new variations, as a dynamic process, temporally divided into segments, of ever new metaphorical transferals and shifts. This process structures the process of understanding as an interplay of optical-acoustic expressive movement, of linguistic signification in the dialog, and of the action represented. (Müller and Kappelhoff 2018, 170)

According to their view on the matter, the terms of cinema's representational systems truly exist only as "residue[s] of [...] events of [metaphorical] figuration" (Andrew 1984, 170). Within this theoretical model, the constant interplay between affective embodiment and the construction of meaning, cinematic expressive movements and the activation of metaphoricity

> [...] structures the time in which the film, through alternating ways of perceiving and various perspectives, reveals itself as a world that follows a logic quite of its own, that is, *a poetic logic* – and not that of our everyday life. [...] For there is no action disclosed to the spectators in an objectively given world, rather there is a subjective world of experience, experienced in concrete ways of perception and forms of sensation. [...] It is a world that in every element is a thought-out and sensed reality. Cinematic metaphors emerge from the affective parcours that viewers go through, they emerge from experiencing the aesthetics of cinematic expressivity. (Müller and Kappelhoff 2018, 172)

If one applies this perspective to SCHLOSS VOGELÖD, the film's dream sequence no longer appears to be a singular figurative event or an erratic stylistic imprint left on the genre of the *Kammerspielfilm* by expressionism. Taken as one element within a larger process of poetic modulation, it instead forms part of the film's overall expressive movement centered around the film's structuring metaphor of a past returning as an alien intrusion from outside – which is itself a variation on the genre's characteristic spatial logic built around the inside-outside division: that the stability of a given community is pressurized by external forces which in turn serve as catalysts for unleashing the destructive power of internal frictions and tensions. Understood as part of an affective course along which Murnau's film takes its spectator, the dream sequence closely corresponds to the rhythms of arrivals and departures; the many tableau-like framings of groups of people and their subtle spatial arrangements of centralization and marginalization; and the alternation of indoor views of the manor and outdoor shots revealing the bad weather coming down on the house to be another external force obstructing the 'normal' course of events.

Furthermore, understood as part of an ongoing modulation of expressive movements shaping the affective experience of a cinematic world unfolding before our eyes, the fact that the dream can be ascribed to a particular character becomes less relevant than the degree to which it contributes to the spectator's (no less subjective) perception and experience of this world. In a purely formalist narratological sense, the fantasy we witness in the dream sequence might appear doubly detached from the represented world first via internal focalization (Branigan 1992, 100–107) and second by comical-ironical distanciation (i.e. it is the clearly pathologized character who is having the nightmare). Phenomenologically, however, it is an integral part of the atmosphere created in SCHLOSS VOGELÖD, or what Müller and Kappelhoff would call its "poetics of affect" when they point out that the "affective resonances" a film generates

> are not identical with the feelings being represented or those of the characters represented. Instead, we are dealing with a complex atmospheric network of mood, extended over time, which only matches up with representational emotions in exceptional cases. It is thus primarily a matter of broad-based affective operations and episodic structures, which are called up and shaped on the part of the spectator through the staging strategies and compositional patterns of audiovisual images. It is in this sense that we speak of a poetics of affect in the ways audiovisual images are presented. (Müller and Kappelhoff 2018, 156)

For Lotte Eisner, it was the creation of affective atmospheres ("Stimmungen") that marked the artistic achievement of Weimar cinema: "In any German film" of the Weimar period, she contends,

> the preoccupation with rendering *Stimmung* ('mood') by suggesting the 'vibrations of the soul' is linked to the use of light. In fact this *Stimmung* hovers around objects as well as people: it is a 'metaphysical' accord, a mystical and singular harmony amid the chaos of things, a kind of sorrowful nostalgia which, for the German, is mixed with well-being, an imprecise nuance of nostalgia, languor coloured with desire, lust of body and soul. (Eisner 2008 [1952], 199)

In particular, Eisner saw *Stimmung* as emanating from the composition of the world presented by the films and from their arrangement and staging of the *Umwelt* of the narrative action – "vibrant with wild poetry, the intensity of which appears to vary proportionately with the ill-fortune falling upon the characters" – as *the* defining characteristic of the *Kammerspielfilm* genre where it "participates 'symphonically' in the action" and, "imbued with a kind of magic, takes on a particular meaning" (Eisner 2008 [1952], 186). It was her keen eye for Murnau's

Figure 2: The menace of a threat lurking on the outside in SCHLOSS VOGELÖD.

subtle maneuverings of *Stimmung* in the visual composition of SCHLOSS VOGELÖD that made her consider the possibility that this particular *Kammerspielfilm* might actually be a horror film in disguise (Eisner 1973, 101). Although she quickly abandons this possibility, she points to the film's atmospheric and affective "Janus faced-ness" communicated less through close-ups of faces to show character emotions than "through attitude and gesture" (Eisner 1973, 102).

Looked at in the light of the previously quoted passage from Müller and Kappelhoff, Eisner's emphasis on the atmospheric dimension of the *Kammerspielfilm* can be re-read as a poetics of affect that reaches far beyond the levels of narrative construction and character emotion.[2] With respect to SCHLOSS VOGELÖD, such an emphasis makes us aware of the degree to which the compositional elements and affective values of the dream sequence are implicated in the overall expressive movement of the film and the spectator's experience of it. Whereas the dream sequence's spatial arrangement can itself be seen as a *pars pro toto* condensation of the larger inside/outside division staged around the Vogelöd manor, the compositions of other scenes inside the house incessantly echo the figurative articulation of the dream sequence by placing individual characters in front of windows through which the bare branches of trees are visible moving in the storm. Their iconic resemblance (transference by similarity) to the slender fingers of the monstrous intruder from the dream sequence thus keeps the menace of a threat lurking on the outside – the film's structuring metaphor – continuously present (Figure 2).

Eloquent gestures, metaphors on the move

Another prominent and closely related compositional element (also highlighted by Eisner) from the dream sequence that keeps returning in other scenes of the film is the gesture of raising an arm towards someone who is already affected – and metaphorically 'touched' – by the shadow it casts over his or her body before there is any physical contact. Although Müller and Kappelhoff are quite clear about the fact that "cinematic expressive movements are not depicted human gestures on the screen", but rather "units of moving audiovision", they do consider the "parallel between gestural and cinematic forms of expressivity [...] as paramount for the analysis and theorizing of cinematic metaphor" (Müller and Kappelhoff 2018, 179). In the context of their model of cinematic metaphor, the act of gestural expression, the body's movement in its concrete temporal

---

[2] For another theoretical revision of the concept of cinematic atmosphere pointing in a similar direction, cf. Sinnerbrink 2012.

articulation, is assumed to be congruent with the course of the spectator's affective experience: "the specific way of performing a gesture *is* the expression of an affective stance" (Müller and Kappelhoff 2018, 148).

This approach to metaphor introduces to the debate a new sensibility for cinema's time-based performative quality, a sensibility already called for by Eisner and one that is especially valuable when dealing with silent film's 'gestural eloquence' (Pearson 1992), so common in Weimar cinema, not least in the work of Murnau. In SCHLOSS VOGELÖD, it is the Baroness who raises her arm and points her finger twice at Count Oetsch (Figure 3): first, when she accuses him in the presence of the assembled hunting party of murdering her first husband and later, at the end of her confession to Father Faramund. Unaware that she is in fact talking to Count Oetsch, she then repeats, in a trance-like state of mind, the same gesture with the words (related by an intertitle): "I accused him of fratricide!"

The second time, her slowly-executed pointing gesture is directed away from Oetsch and outside the image; however, the shadow that slowly comes into view with the raising of her arm rips straight into the heart of the man whose true identity is thereby revealed. This calculated effect of the scene's staging and lighting through which the shadow seems to emancipate itself from its metonymical ties to the Baroness's limb – in the act of the movement itself – assumes a metaphorical existence, disrupting the scene's semantic field and radically shifting its meaning. It is the expressive movement – both physically and cinematically – of the outstretched arm and its shadow that establishes another metaphorical relationship between the guilty woman and the monstrous nocturnal intruder, between the dream sequence and the rest of the film.

In contrast to many of their predecessors who, in the wake of Christian Metz, formulated their theories of metaphoricity in film with reference to individual auteurs (such as Eisenstein or Buñuel) or stylistic innovations of historical film movements such as German expressionism, Soviet montage cinema or French surrealism, Müller and Kappelhoff's theory of cinematic metaphor is more comprehensive and unbiased when it comes to the analysis of popular genre cinema. As the example of Murnau's SCHLOSS VOGELÖD indicates, neither cinematic expressionism nor the genre of the *Kammerspielfilm* are clearly distinguishable categories but form instead flexible configurations in specific historical situations. Tracing the migration of cinematic expressive movements and the transformation of the metaphorical meanings they carry with them across generical and cultural contexts is another promising perspective this approach opens up.

Within the oeuvre of Murnau alone, this pattern of trans-generic migration and transformation can be shown in manifold ways. If one considers the dream sequence from SCHLOSS VOGELÖD, one notices immediately that it provides

Figure 3: The Baroness pointing her finger twice at Count Oetsch in SCHLOSS VOGELÖD.

the compositional blueprint for the scene from NOSFERATU (Friedrich Wilhelm Murnau, GER 1922; the film Murnau made right after SCHLOSS VOGELÖD) in which the vampire Count Orlok aka Nosferatu approaches Hutter, a guest at his castle in Transylvania, at night, his mighty shadow falling over the body of the flinching young man in bed (Figure 4).

Figure 4: Nosferatu's mighty shadow falling over the body of the flinching Hutter in bed (NOSFERATU).

A second scene from NOSFERATU, the dramatic climax of the film when Ellen invites Count Orlok to her bedroom in Bremerhaven, sends Hutter away, and sacrifices herself to the vampire, not only echoes the first scene in Transylvania insofar as it is again the vampire's shadow that falls first on the surroundings and finally on the body of his victim (Figure 5). In that it is the shadow of the vampire's hand, closing his fist around the heart of Ellen who is squirming with pain, the expressive movement here adds to the composition the metaphorical logic of the shadow pointing in the opposite direction of the arm of the Baroness, hitting Count Oetsch straight in the heart.

Another example that develops this expressive movement pattern even further can be found in a key scene from Murnau's version of FAUST (Friedrich

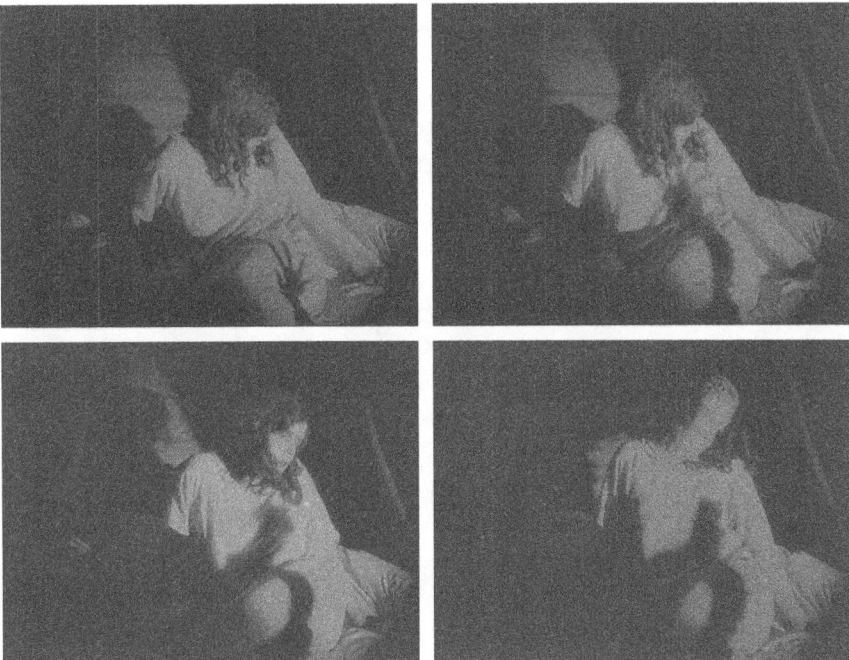

Figure 5: Nosferatu's shadow falling on Hutter's fiancé Ellen (NOSFERATU).

Wilhelm Murnau, GER 1926), made four years after NOSFERATU. Led by Mephisto, Faust pays Gretchen a surprise visit at night. Although this is the moment in the film which marks the climax of Faust's rise to bliss and happiness, the scene already carries signs of doom, for it is the child that is fathered that night that sets into motion the tragedy of Gretchen. A closer analysis of this scene would result in a number of striking analogies to the scene in which Ellen sacrifices herself to Nosferatu: Mephisto's huge shadow falling on the house in the beginning; Gretchen's white nightgown and her opening and closing of the window; Faust's forced entry into the room with his silhouetted hands pushing the window open and echoing the predatory gesture with which Nosferatu approaches both Hutter and Ellen (Figure 6).[3]

---

[3] Similar visual configurations are to be found in Murnau's work up to SUNRISE – A SONG OF TWO HUMANS (USA 1927) – which appears almost as a remake of FAUST when judged on the basis of its compositional patterns – and his last film TABU (USA 1930), which is full of compositional allusions to NOSFERATU.

Figure 6: Faust's forced entry into Gretchen's room (FAUST).

Such compositional resonances can, of course, simply be regarded as indicative of Murnau's consistency in directorial style. But, understood through Müller and Kappelhoff's theory of cinematic metaphor, the migration of cinematic expressive movements also allows one to see a basic similarity and gradual shift in the metaphorical organization and affective poetics underpinning the genres of the *Kammerspielfilm* and the Fantastic in Weimar cinema. At any rate, Murnau's fantasy films of the Weimar period share with their *Kammerspielfilm* counterparts a world structured around inside/outside divisions, often marked by architectural elements such as walls, doors, and windows; violent invasive movements of external forces into existing environments and communities (Vogelöd castle, Bremerhaven in NOSFERATU, Gretchen's village in FAUST); the unmistakably sexual connotation that comes with these penetrations of private spaces; and the transformative power of shadows and silhouettes turning the bodies of their carriers figuratively (and, at least in the case of Nosferatu, also literally) into something else altogether. Reconstructing from these figurations of cinematic metaphoricity, and from the affective resonances they produce, the signature of Weimar cinema's historicity beyond the stylistic formula of expressionism and across individual oeuvres and genres would provide a promising complement to Müller and Kappelhoff's valuable theoretical template of cinematic metaphor.

Audiovisual sources

DAS CABINET DES DR. CALIGARI [THE CABINET OF DR. CALIGARI], Dir. Robert Wiene. Decla-Bioscop, GER 1920.
SCHLOSS VOGELÖD [THE HAUNTED CASTLE], Dir. Friedrich Wilhelm Murnau. Uco-Film, GER 1921.
NOSFERATU – EINE SYMPHONIE DES GRAUENS [NOSFERATU], Dir. Friedrich Wilhelm Murnau. Prana-Film, GER 1922.
SCHATTEN [WARNING SHADOWS], Dir. Arthur Robison, Pan-Film, GER 1923.
FAUST – EINE DEUTSCHE VOLKSSAGE [FAUST], Dir. Friedrich Wilhelm Murnau. UFA, GER 1926.
METROPOLIS, Dir. Fritz Lang. UFA, GER 1927.
SUNRISE – A SONG OF TWO HUMANS, Dir. Friedrich Wilhelm Murnau. Fox Film Corporation, USA 1927.
TABU – A STORY OF THE SOUTH SEAS, Dir. Friedrich Wilhelm Murnau. Paramount Pictures, USA 1931.

Bibliography

Andrew, Dudley. 1984. *Concepts in Film Theory*. Oxford: Oxford University Press.
Branigan, Edward. 1992. *Narrative Comprehension and Film*. London: Routledge.
Budd, Mike. 1990. "Moments of Caligari." In *The Cabinet of Dr. Caligari. Texts, Contexts, Histories*, edited by Mike Budd, 7–121. New Brunswick: Rutgers University Press.
Choe, Steve. 2014. *Afterlives. Allegories of Film and Mortality in Early Weimar Germany*. New York, NY: Bloomsbury.
Eisner, Lotte H. 1973. *Murnau*. London: Secker & Warburg.
Eisner, Lotte H. 2008. *The Haunted Screen. Expressionism in the German Cinema and the Influence of Max Reinhardt*. Translated by Roger Greaves. Berkeley, CA: University of California Press. Original edition 1952.
Elsaesser, Thomas. 2000. *Weimar Cinema and After. Germany's Historical Imaginary*. London: Routledge.
Henry, Michael. 1971. *Le Cinéma Expressioniste Allemand. Un Langage Métaphorique*. Fribourg: Editions du Signe.
Jakobson, Roman. 1971. "Two Aspects of Language and Two Types of Aphasic Disturbances." In *Fundamentals of Language*, 69–96. The Hague: De Gruyter Mouton. Original edition 1956.
Kaplan, E. Ann. 1998. "The 'Dark Continent' of Film Noir. Race, Displacement and Metaphor in Tourneur's *Cat People* (1942) and Welles' *The Lady from Shanghai* (1948)." In *Women in Film Noir*, edited by E. Ann Kaplan, 83–201. London: BFI Publishing.
Kracauer, Siegfried. 1947. *From Caligari to Hitler. A Psychological History of German Film*. Princeton, NJ: Princeton University Press.
Metz, Christian. 1982. *Psychoanalysis and Cinema. The Imaginary Signifier*. London: Macmillan Press.

Müller, Cornelia, and Hermann Kappelhoff. 2018. *Cinematic Metaphor. Experience – Affectivity – Temporality*. In collaboration with Sarah Greifenstein, Dorothea Horst, Thomas Scherer, and Christina Schmitt. Berlin/Boston, MA: Walter de Gruyter.

Naremore, James. 2008. *More than Night. Film Noir in Its Contexts*. Berkeley, CA: University of California Press.

Pearson, Roberta E. 1992. *Eloquent Gestures. The Transformation of Performance Style in the Griffith Biograph Films*. Berkeley, CA: University of California Press.

Ropars-Wuilleumier, Marie-Claire. 1978. "The Function of Metaphor in Eisenstein's 'October'." *Film Criticism* 2 (2): 109–127.

Sadowski, Piotr. 2018. *The Semiotics of Light and Shadows. Modern Visual Arts and Weimar Cinema*. London: Bloomsbury.

Scheunemann, Dietrich. 2003. "The Double, the Décor, and the Framing Device. Once More on Robert Wiene's *The Cabinet of Dr. Caligari*." In *Expressionist Film. New Perspectives*, edited by Dietrich Scheunemann, 125–56. Rochester: Camden House.

Sinnerbrink, Robert. 2012. "*Stimmung*. Exploring the Aesthetics of Mood." *Screen* 53 (2): 148–163.

Whittock, Trevor. 1990. *Metaphor and Film*. Cambridge: Cambridge University Press.

Williams, Linda. 1976. "The Prologue to *Un Chien Andalou*. A Surrealist Film Metaphor." *Screen* 17 (4): 24–33.

Williams, Linda. 1981a. "Dream Rhetoric and Film Rhetoric. Metaphor and Metonymy in *Un Chien Andalou*." *Semiotica* 33 (1–2): 87–103.

Williams, Linda. 1981b. *Figures of Desire. A Theory and Analysis of Surrealist Film*. Berkeley, CA: University of California Press.

Alan Cienki
Insights for Linguistics and Gesture Studies from Film Studies: A View from Researching Cinematic Metaphor

Introduction

Identifying and interpreting possible metaphors in film is far more complex than doing so with a text of individual words on a page, as this volume and its precursor (Müller and Kappelhoff 2018) make clear. The simultaneous and sequential composition of verbal and visual elements of many kinds in films confronts the researcher with a multidimensional puzzle that can have multiple solutions. Yet, while a conversation captured on video for the purposes of linguistic analysis is normally a far cry from a high budget, commercially produced feature film, both the linguist researching spoken language and the film scholar are viewing 'motion pictures' in order to understand something about the human use of semiotic resources in a communicative context. Attention to metaphoric expression provides a special lens through which the analytic processes involved can be brought into focus.

This chapter begins with some starting points for thinking about the study of language from an audiovisual perspective. Here the inherent dynamicity of metaphor use in cinema provides a particular point of entry for reflection on what one considers relevant processes of meaning making, as well as how one can analyze and interpret them. This allows for the consideration of general processes of how semantic interpretation can be conducted in regard to language, when face-to-face communication is viewed in its dynamic and variably multimodal complexity. We then turn some aesthetic attention to ways in which gestures give form to ideas, including the process in which the abstract is made more tangible through metaphoric use of gestures. The possible perspectives one can have on embodied communication deserve special attention here. Finally, we consider how giving greater consideration to the poetics of everyday practices can play a role in helping contemporary linguistics and gesture studies (re)claim a place as fields of study rooted in the humanities.

Linguistics, cognitive linguistics, and gesture studies

A main concern of a cognitively-oriented approach to linguistics is how the forms of language – in general and in terms of individual languages – can provide insight into how people conceptualize the world – in general and in given "usage events" (Langacker 1988) of language-based communication. What is now known as conceptual metaphor theory, along with theoretical approaches concerned with mental spaces and conceptual integration, frames, force dynamics, cognitive grammar, and other notions, constituted the foundational fields of research for what became cognitive linguistics (see Geeraerts and Cuyckens 2007 for an overview). One characteristic that cognitive linguistic approaches have in common is that they are usage-based (Barlow and Kemmer 2000), meaning that they take actual language usage as evidence of linguistic knowledge. While this may sound unextraordinary to someone new to linguistics, in fact, this premise goes against the methodological practice, and theoretical bases, of what has remained the dominant school of linguistics in North America and many other parts of the world since the second half of the twentieth century, namely generative linguistics, in its various incarnations (Harris 1993). The framework of generative linguistics considers the distinction between people's linguistic competence (implicit knowledge of a language's grammar) and their linguistic performance (the way in which they actually utter phrases in the language) to be a fundamental one from a theoretical point of view. According to this view, since performance can involve many kinds of factors (memory limitations, interruptions from sneezing or coughing, etc.), it is not an accurate reflection of one's linguistic competence (Chomsky 1965, 3). Competence is then studied by implicit means, such as by asking native speakers of a language whether certain variants of constructed sentences conform with their intuitions about what is grammatical in their language or not. Partly through the dominance of this approach in many academic institutions, the study of language use migrated to find a home in other fields, such as sociology (witness the rise of conversation analysis as a sub-field of sociology) and cultural anthropology (where the ethnography of speaking [later named "the ethnography of communication"] developed).

Despite the turn in cognitive (and, in general, functionally oriented) approaches to taking language use as the object of study, cognitive linguistics is still under the sway of a written language bias that permeates linguistic theorizing (Linell 2005) in general. Although there is ostensible neutrality with respect to the mode of the language being studied, the norms of written language still serve as the tacit default when referring to linguistic forms. In the twenty first century there has been increasing attention given to studying spoken language usage events (Cienki 2015b) in their own right, particularly when it comes to research on grammatical constructions (e.g., Carter and McCarthy 1995, Du Bois 2014), but the complexity of the linguistic reality that comes to light with the use of video recordings of talk data has only begun to be explored (see the work on the issue of multimodality in relation to grammar, e.g., Fricke 2012, Ladewig 2014, Schoonjans 2014, Zima and Bergs 2017).

From the perspective of cognitive linguistics, behaviors in talk-based communication serve as cues by which interlocutors construct best attempts at each other's meanings (see Fillmore 1985 and Langacker 1987). On this basis, gestural movements, so often tied as they are to speakers' utterances, also demand attention as material to be studied in order to gain a more complete picture of how language reflects aspects of speakers' conceptualizations (Cienki 2013a). Indeed, gesture research is gaining a central place as a sub-field in cognitive linguistics, as is evidenced by the regularity of gesture panels being included in cognitive linguistics conferences, and the number of articles including data from gesture being published in journals like *Cognitive Linguistics*.

Weighing different time scales

While looking at videos as data is a familiar practice in fields like anthropology, in which visual anthropology has come to be a respected area of specialization, in linguistics, beyond research on sign languages, it is still relatively novel. Indeed, using video as data certainly brings a novel perspective to linguistic research. One factor that it highlights is language as a phenomenon that is dynamic at its core in terms of its moment-to-moment use. This fact, something that is central to the study of films, is one which can be (and usually is) easily overlooked in the field of linguistics as a consequence of the practice of reifying language for study in its written form.

Linguists tend to focus on the basic levels of linguistic experience (see the foundational research in Rosch et al. 1976 on levels of categorization). The relevant levels are traditionally considered those of meaningful sounds in a language (phonemes), meaning-bearing parts of words (morphemes), grammatical phrase structures and clauses (syntactic structures), with sentences being the highest-level unit that many linguists deem relevant for their analysis. However, *listening to* language use already reveals overarching layers of structure in the form of prosodic patterns of intonation, changes in volume, use of pauses, etc. These contribute a higher-level structure to the "basic level" of language use. Going further, *looking at* language use, shows the additional higher level structures of patterns of gestural emphasis with rhythmic beat gestures and repeated use of gesture forms or locations in space that can link ideas across portions of discourse, as with discourse-cohesive gestures (McNeill and Levy 1993) or so-called gestural "catchments" (McNeill et al. 2001). These reveal that the meaning-structures being expressed are constituted on multiple time scales – some smaller, on the level at which we utter morphemes, and some larger, on the level of discourse structures – and the latter are invisible to researchers if only audio or, even more extreme, only written transcripts of the talk are taken into consideration.

Let us adopt Clark's (1996, 21) term of "attender" for anyone paying attention to the speaker – a term which removes the conundrum of whether there is an intended addressee who actually may not be the one listening to or viewing the speaker. When trying to interpret the linguistic and gestural forms used in a communicative context, as any attenders present would have encountered them, not just any time scale can be used for interpreting them. Rather, the actual time scale of production is the one relevant for the human experience of language use. While slow motion (especially with repeated viewings) can be helpful for seeing and hearing details of behavioral features that may slip past our conscious perception of the video recording, and higher speed playback may help perceive larger scale patterns over time (see below), analyses from slow and high speed viewings can tell us more about what an *ideal* attender might have perceived and understood in that context than what the *actual* attender present may have picked up (see also the issue of perspectives, discussed below). It is worth bearing in mind that these "problems" of being able to consider viewing human behavior on much slower or faster time scales did not even exist before the invention of film recording, and did not become a common part of the broader public's experience in industrialized cultures until access to digital video and convenient devices for playing it became widespread. For example, even Merleau-Ponty's extensive discussion of temporality in his *Phenomenology of Perception* (2002 [1945]) does not consider slow motion or accelerated time scales in relation to the everyday lived time scale.

The view of language as fundamentally temporally organized (on the time scale of its production and comprehension as well as on micro levels of articulatory detail and on macro levels of diachronic language change) also facilitates viewing language not as an isolated module, but as one semiotic system for communication that is used along with others. This includes acknowledging that the linguistic system is used variably with other semiotic codes (especially gesture, but also sometimes others, such as illustration/drawing) that rely on different means of production and perception than spoken language does (with different articulators for motoric production, and more reliance on the visual mode for perception). We can therefore call language-based communication variably multimodal, with the nature of the variability itself varying on various time scales (Cienki 2012, 2015a, 2017b).

With the audiovisual approach to studying language-based communication discussed here, we see that it involves not only sequential patterns, but also simultaneous forms of expression. This is something that was seen as impossible with a 'linear' view of language. Chomsky (2007, 65) writes, "The articulatory and perceptual systems, for example, require that expressions of the language have a linear (temporal, 'left-to-right') order at the interface; sensorimotor systems that operated in parallel would allow richer modes of expression of higher dimensionality". The hypothetical situation raised in the second half of the quote, however, is precisely the situation we find with gesture and speech. The simultaneity of expression that becomes apparent as we look at video recordings of talk as data for linguistic analysis has to do not only with the combination of speech and gesture, but also with the multiple layers of complexity that are superimposed on each other. Video analysis of talk helps reveal the multiple levels playing out at once. For the linguist, considering data analysis in light of film analysis raises fundamental questions about what it means for linguists to do semantic analysis: if the language they are examining as data is not isolated words on a page, but is behavior in contextualized use playing out on a human timescale, then it inherently overlaps in variable ways with other simultaneously produced audio and/or visual expressions from other semiotic systems. Kendon (2004) provides one solution by resorting to the higher level of "utterance", referring to gesture in his later work as "utterance dedicated visible bodily action" (Kendon 2015, 44), leaving implicit the conclusion that speech is then utterance dedicated audible (but also often visible) bodily action.

The poetics of everyday, utterance dedicated actions

Consideration of the study of cinematic metaphor also sheds light on broader issues for the study of face-to-face language use. While it has long been argued that linguistic and poetic approaches to the study of language have much to gain from each other's perspectives (Jakobson 1960), Chafe (2008) takes the argument further, observing that analyzing spoken language usage has affinities with music and art appreciation. Repeated playing of the audio recordings for purposes of transcription and analysis can result in a distancing from it, an estrangement (*ostraneniye*), as Shklovskiy (1929) called it (a neologism in Russian from the root *stran-* 'strange'). Indeed, it is this process which he claims is at the heart of art:

> The goal of art is to give the feeling of a thing as a vision, not as a recognition; the technique of art is the technique of 'ostraneniye' of things and the technique of the form made difficult, magnifying the difficulty and length of apprehension, since the process of apprehension in

art is autotelic and should be extended; *art is the means of experiencing the doing of a thing, and the already-done in art is not important.*"[1] (Shklovskiy 1929, 13, emphasis in original, translation by A.C.).

Returning to the context of video analysis of talk as data, this momentary estrangement from the material being analyzed allows for such an aesthetic stance towards it. Perhaps this is even more the case when the data is not just an audio-recording but is video material. It can result in a kind of aestheticizing of the everyday, as discussed in Light and Smith (2005) and Leddy (2012). The close-up, detailed examination of the speakers' movements in relation to their talk, often done using slow motion for more fine-grained viewing of details, can induce a performative view of human behavior. Taking an aesthetic stance towards gestural details sometimes highlights their qualities as dance-like, particularly when video data is viewed with the sound turned off, as is sometimes done in order to focus on gesture form and movement qualities when coding them for purposes of categorization (e.g., Bressem 2013).

A case in point is the different gestural modes of representation (Müller 1998a, b, 2014) or depiction (Streeck 2008, 2009, ch. 6). Manual gestures whose forms and/or movements can be seen to be in an iconic relation with aspects of the entities, relations, or processes mentioned in the speech or pragmatically understood from the discourse context (such as reference to a topic mentioned earlier) can be represented by one or a combination of four modes of representation. Though sometimes named in different ways in the literature, they basically involve the following (elaborating on Müller's [1998a, b] original explication). An illustration of each of these can be seen in the appendix of this chapter. Each of these modes can involve one or both hands.

a) The hand performing an action like it would in a given context, *re-enacting* it, but without the actual objects that it might manipulate.
b) The hand is positioned and/or moves as if *touching* or holding the surface of an object, thereby showing features of its size and/or shape.
c) The hand *embodies* the thing itself, such as a flat object with a flat hand, or a roundish one with a fist.
d) An extended finger or fingers of the hand move so that the tip(s) of the finger(s) *traces* or draws a form.

---

[1] "Целью искусства является дать ощущение вещи, как видение, а не как узнавание; приемом искусства является прием «остранения» вещей и прием затрудненной формы, увеличивающий трудность и долготу восприятия, так как восприемательный процесс в искусстве самоцелен и должен быть продлен; искусство есть способ пережить деланье вещи, а сделанное в искусстве не важно" (note that in the original Russian, the words translated into English as "doing" and "done" are ambiguous with "making" and "made").

The modes can also interact; e.g., the hand that is as-if touching the surface of an object could also be seen as embodying that surface itself.

It is now well known that representational and deictic gestures are employed in reference to abstract domains as well, which has been argued to constitute metaphor in gesture (see, for example, Cienki 2013b, Cienki and Müller 2008a, b, 2014): rendering the abstract in the physical form of gesture already casts the target concept in terms of a spatial, imagistic form with which it is being compared. While concepts of the physical can also be recast metaphorically in terms of another domain in gesture (e.g., Fricke's, 2007, 180, example of calling someone an ass [*Esel* in German] while holding up fingers next to each of their own ears to represent the animal's ears), such examples appear to occur rarely in natural conversation.

The following are some examples, attested in previous research, that illustrate how the four modes of representation can be used metaphorically in reference to abstract domains.

a) People in various cultures have been shown to talk about considering the importance of different ideas as if they were holding objects on their palm-up open hands, moving the hands up and down in alternation, enacting how they would assess the weight of each object (Cienki 1998, 193–194).
b) A speaker may talk about an abstract realm (like the domain of education) while holding one's slightly curved hands, palms facing each other, slightly apart, as if there were a somewhat rounded object between them (Cienki 2013c, 675).
c) In many cultures, people enumerate points in an argument while sequentially extending or touching individual fingers on one hand with their other hand, as if the fingers were (as if they embodied) the points they were discussing (Sweetser 1998).
d) People may be talking about different ways of acting in a situation, and how deciding between what is right or wrong is like having to "draw your line", while simultaneously tracing a vertical line in the air to illustrate this (Cienki 2010).

In all these cases, the body itself constitutes a medium of expression, representing ideas, even based on abstract concepts, in terms of spatial forms and movements. Questions that remain for future research about the representation of ideas spatially in gestural form in any given culture include whether speakers gesture about physical and abstract concepts with equal frequency or not, and whether the forms of the gestures they use for physical and abstract (metaphoric) referents are similar or different in form. Answers to both of these questions (explored in Müller 2010, 2016, and Tong [in preparation], for example) can provide insights into similarities and differences in how speakers of a given language conceptualize, and presumably mentally simulate in some way, concepts of the physical and (metaphorically) of the abstract (Hostetter and Alibali 2008, Marghetis and Bergen 2014; see Gibbs' contribution to this volume for more on the issue of mental simulation in relation to cinematic experience and metaphor).

Appreciating the poetics of everyday behavior, such as the artistic quality or clever imaginativeness of a metaphoric gesture, is normally squelched in the move from the research process (e.g., in anecdotal observations of inter-individual differences in research participants' gestural behavior) to the research output. This is either because it is usually not deemed relevant to the research question that one began with, or the observation is not seen as one that could be operationalized in a sufficiently objective way to fit in with the scientific method. This is not surprising if one considers the assumptions of (and aspirations to) objectivity in "the" scientific method that spread from the natural sciences to the social and behavioral sciences, and the historical shift in focus in Western (and particularly Anglo-American) aesthetics from all kinds of phenomena to the confines of the fine arts (Saito 2015).

Nevertheless, gesture research sometimes gives rise to moments of spontaneous appreciation of the qualities of the gesturing hand form or its movement, as the researcher disengages from trained purposive responses to viewing what is transpiring in the video as data and finds oneself experiencing a state of "aesthetic attention" (Hausman 1989, 134, building on Kant 1902 [1790]). Here, "Attention to its object becomes intransitive rather than transitive" (Hausman 1989, 135). Referring to what would more traditionally be considered works of art, Hausman (1989, 136) writes, "This positive aspect of the object of aesthetic attention is to be found in the internal relations of the object's components". Viewing gestures, aesthetic attention can lead to productive "ostraneniye" from the object of inquiry, as realization of the intricacy of its nature becomes magnified as the length of time with which it is apprehended is lengthened, to paraphrase Shklovskiy's characterization above.

Acknowledgment of such moments in the process of research can afford exploiting them for new insights. In the study of movement quality of gestures, some colleagues and I involved in a recent project (Cienki and Iriskhanova, in press) found the relevant gesture coding categories we were using to be easily interpretable in terms of vocalized sounds. The categories had to do with whether a pulse of effort was involved in the gesture production, or whether the gesture involved more sustained control of effort throughout the movement. This distinction was intuitive for some of us in terms of a pulse of effort in vocalization (with a burst of volume and marked pitch contour) versus feeling and giving voice to a more sustained, even pitch and volume when seeing gestures that lacked the pulse of effort. Discussion of this led to better understanding not only of what constituted a pulse of effort in gestures, but also insights into the relation of effort pulses in gesture with prosodic peaks in the speech (cf. the view of the manual movement and speech production systems as being coupled oscillators; Iverson and Thelen 1999).

First, second, and third person perspectives

It is worth bearing in mind the three perspectives that are involved when recorded human interaction constitutes one's data for research (on gesture or other factors). An attender may be playing any one of these roles, however, due to cognitive constraints: only one role in any given moment, although alternation between perspectives is possible (just as one can normally only view the optical illusion of a vase and two opposing faces as one or the other at any given moment, though one can quickly alternate between seeing the illusion one way or the other). As discussed in Cienki (2017a, 136), the perspectives are as follows:
1. That of the first-person role of producer of the gestural, verbal, or other behavior.
2. That of an observer in the context, which includes the second-person role of the intended addressee, but also that of a passer-by, an eavesdropper, etc. (as discussed in Clark 1996, Chapter 1).
3. The third-person role of one hearing and/or viewing the behavior or a recording of it, an attender, at a later time, and likely in a different place, than that in which it was produced. A film viewer and/or researcher and a gesture researcher both take on this role in relation to their material of study.

It is important for the researcher to make clear which of these perspectives they are making claims about with their analysis. For example, if some words, gestures, other embodied expressions, or images/pictures are being claimed to be metaphorically used, the question is, from whose perspective? In metaphor research about communicative behaviors produced by people who are not in the role of actor, claims about the third perspective can, wittingly or unwittingly, be conflated with claims about the first perspective, which is unfortunate in that evidence-based analysis can become conflated with what appears to be mind-reading. A related question is: To what degree are one's claims about what *ideal* attenders rather than what *actual* attenders, in situ or after the fact, may have made out of any communicative event? With regard to this question, the Chomskian construct of the ideal speaker-listener, explicitly referenced in generative linguistic theorizing ("Linguistic theory is concerned primarily with an ideal speaker-listener"; Chomsky 1965, 3), can still be found sometimes implicitly playing a role in cognitive linguistic research.

The third-person perspective is the one which might be argued to normally best facilitate assuming aesthetic attention. However, the characterization of the third-person role can also be applied to the first and second roles above, in which case the "at a later time" can even mean during a repetition of the behavior (words uttered or gesture made) by oneself or by an other attender in context, perhaps explicitly to give aesthetic attention to the action itself. Compare what Tannen (1989, 64) calls "savoring" in conversation: appreciation can be showed of someone's (maybe even one's own) use of humor or irony by repeating words that someone (perhaps just recently) uttered, possibly imitating their vocal style in order to display and enjoy the qualities, as well as the possible import, of what was so uttered. One can imagine the same kind of repetition of gestures produced for similar purposes of savoring. Aesthetic attention is thus not limited to after-the-fact viewing of recorded communication events (films or videos of unscripted interactions or events) by outsiders, but can also be experienced by first or second-person participants in the events themselves as they are taking place.

Minding our poetics

The study of metaphor in film, spoken language, and/or gesture can be approached either in terms of questions from cognitive science, arguably placing it more on the side of the social sciences, or in terms of poetic and aesthetic (in the broad sense) concerns, fitting in more with what is traditionally considered the humanistic side of academic inquiry. The physiologist, psychologist, and linguist Tatyana Chernígovskaya (2016) claimed in an interview, "All forms of art describe what is human out of what is human."[2] Ironically, this definition does not apply as directly to some types of films (such as those produced from computer animation), while for those based on stories of people shown as people, the connection is more obvious. However, the above characterization of art has no problem being applied to gesture, sign language, and spoken language. Gesture has been argued to reflect, to varying degrees, humans' spatio-motoric concepts in a human, embodied form – whether for concepts of the physical or for concepts of the abstract realized metaphorically via concrete domains, as illustrated above in the use of the gestural modes of representation. Signed, spoken, and written

---

[2] "Все виды исскуства описывают человеческое из человеческого" (translation by A.C.).

languages also express our concepts in embodied form and for a wider range of concepts than just the spatio-motoric. In that sense, language can be seen as gesture that is perceived either through its resultant visual forms, sounds, or written traces (Armstrong, Stokoe, and Wilcox 1995). Language renders concepts in the embodied forms of articulatory movements, but with much more explicitly normalized forms than those of most spontaneously produced gestures, allowing for conventional symbolization of a much wider range of concepts (with the term "concepts" here meant to also encompass perceptual and affective experiences). In this sense, gesture and language, also like many kinds of cinema, describe what is human out of what is human.

Lakoff and Johnson (1980) popularized the idea that metaphor is not primarily a matter of poetic expression, but rather is characteristic of everyday thought. Gibbs (1994) and Turner (1996), like Jakobson (1956) much earlier, argued that phenomena we recognize as metaphor and metonymy are but more salient examples of basic ways in which the mind works. These points about how our cognitive processes have what we might call poetic roots, that we see in everyday language use, were fundamental ones that helped give rise to the field of cognitive linguistics. But now we can argue that there is also value in looking in the opposite direction: at how empirical research in cognitive linguistics can gain new insights if aesthetic attention is given to the phenomena under examination. In this regard, and surely in others, linguistics – and particularly cognitive linguistics, located as it is between the humanities and the social sciences – can benefit from assuming a balanced position that takes its roots in the humanities into greater account.

Appendix: Examples of gestural modes of representation

The examples of gestural modes of representation, adapted from the original characterizations in Müller (1998a, b), are drawn from research by Wu (in preparation). They come from the UCLA Library Broadcast NewsScape and were accessed via the facilities of the Distributed Little Red Hen Lab (redhenlab.org), a program co-directed by Francis Steen and Mark Turner. For each example, the words in square brackets are the ones that were uttered while the speaker produced the gesture (during the gesture "stroke") and held it afterwards, if at all.

a) The hand performs an action like it would in a given context, *re-enacting* it, but without the actual objects that it might manipulate.

Here the speaker is holding her hands as if they are clasping an object and moving them outward when talking about handing someone a piece of paper: she is describing being stopped in her car by a police officer who asked for her driver's license, which she gave to him (Figure 1).

Figure 1: "so I [gave him my license]".

b) The hand is positioned and/or moves as if *touching* or holding the surface of an object, thereby showing the object's features, such as size and/or shape.

Here the speaker is holding his hands open and apart, palms facing each other, when talking about holding a pair of wooden shoes that his father brought to him as a gift from Holland (Figure 2).

Figure 2: "and he had brought me some.., some uh [wooden shoes]".

c) The hand *embodies* the thing itself.
Here the speaker is holding out his left hand, flat, palm up, when talking about a CD (Figure 3).

Figure 3: "every one of those guys brought [me a CD of mine, to sign for 'em]".

An extended finger or fingers of the hand move so that the tip(s) of the finger(s) *traces* or draws a form.
Here the speaker is dragging the tip of his index finger across his upper lip and talking about a mustache (Figure 4).

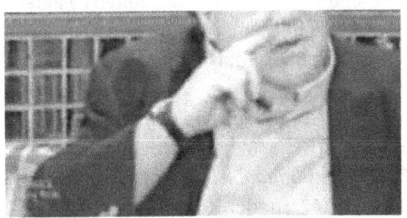

Figure 4: "and given [me John's mustache]".

Bibliography

Armstrong, David F., William C. Stokoe, and Sherman E. Wilcox. 1995. *Gesture and the Nature of Language*. Cambridge: Cambridge University Press.

Barlow, Michael, and Suzanne Kemmer, eds. 2000. *Usage-based Models of Language*. Stanford, CA: CSLI Publications.

Bressem, Jana. 2013. "A Linguistic Perspective on the Notation of Form Features in Gestures." In *Body – Language – Communication. An International Handbook on Multimodality in Human Interaction*, edited by Cornelia Müller, Alan Cienki, Ellen Fricke, Silva Ladewig, David McNeill, and Sedinha Teßendorf, 1079–1098. Berlin: De Gruyter Mouton.

Carter, Ronald, and Michael McCarthy. 1995. "Grammar and Spoken Language." *Applied Linguistics* 16 (2): 141–158.
Chafe, Wallace. 2008. "Aspects of Discourse Analysis." *Brno Studies in English* 34 (1): 23–37.
Chernigovskaya, Tatyana Vladimirovna. 2016. Interview by Vladimir Pozner. *Pozner*, 11 April 2016, www.1tv.ru/shows/pozner/vypuski/gost-tatyana-chernigovskaya-pozner-vypusk-ot-11042016. Accessed 29 December 2017.
Chomsky, Noam. 1965. *Aspects of the Theory of Syntax*. Cambridge, MA: MIT Press.
Chomsky, Noam. 2007. "Language and Thought. Descartes and Some Reflections on Venerable Themes." In *The Prehistory of Cognitive Science*, edited by Andrew Brook, 38–66. London: Palgrave.
Cienki, Alan. 1998. "Metaphoric Gestures and Some of Their Relations to Verbal Metaphoric Expressions." In *Discourse and Cognition. Bridging the Gap*, edited by Jean-Pierre Koenig, 189–204. Stanford, CA: CSLI Publications.
Cienki, Alan. 2010. "Multimodal Metaphor Analysis." In *Metaphor Analysis. Research Practice in Applied Linguistics, Social Sciences and the Humanities*, edited by Lynne Cameron and Robert Maslen, 195–214. London: Equinox.
Cienki, Alan. 2012. "Usage Events of Spoken Language and the Symbolic Units We (May) Abstract from Them." In *Cognitive Processes in Language*, edited by Janusz Badio and Krzysztof Kosecki, 149–158. Bern: Peter Lang.
Cienki, Alan. 2013a. "Cognitive Linguistics. Spoken Language and Gesture as Expressions of Conceptualization." In *Body – Language – Communication. An International Handbook on Multimodality in Human Interaction*, edited by Cornelia Müller, Alan Cienki, Ellen Fricke, Silva Ladewig, David McNeill, and Sedinha Teßendorf, 182–201. Berlin: De Gruyter Mouton.
Cienki, Alan. 2013b. "Conceptual Metaphor Theory in Light of Research on Gesture with Speech." *Cognitive Semiotics* 5 (1–2): 349–366.
Cienki, Alan. 2013c. "Gesture, Space, Grammar, and Cognition." In *Space in Language and Linguistics. Geographical, Interactional, and Cognitive Perspectives*, edited by Peter Auer, Martin Hilpert, Anja Stukenbrock, and Benedikt Szmrecsanyi, 667–686. Berlin: De Gruyter.
Cienki, Alan. 2015a. "Repetitions in View of Talk as Variably Multimodal." *Vestnik of Moscow State Linguistic University* 6 (717): 625–634.
Cienki, Alan. 2015b. "Spoken Language Usage Events." *Language and Cognition* 7: 499–514.
Cienki, Alan. 2017a. "Analysing Metaphor in Gesture. A Set of Metaphor Identification Guidelines for Gesture (MIG-G)." In *The Routledge Handbook of Metaphor and Language*, edited by Elena Semino and Zsófia Demjén, 131–147. London: Routledge.
Cienki, Alan. 2017b. *Ten Lectures on Spoken Language and Gesture from the Perspective of Cognitive Linguistics. Issues of Dynamicity and Multimodality*. Leiden: Brill.
Cienki, Alan, and Olga Iriskhanova, eds. *Aspectuality Across Languages. Event Construal in Speech and Gesture*. Amsterdam: Benjamins, in press.
Cienki, Alan, and Cornelia Müller, eds. 2008a. *Metaphor and Gesture*. Amsterdam: John Benjamins.
Cienki, Alan, and Cornelia Müller. 2008b. "Metaphor, Gesture, and Thought." In *The Cambridge Handbook of Metaphor and Thought*, edited by Raymond W. Jr. Gibbs, 483–501. Cambridge: Cambridge University Press.
Cienki, Alan, and Cornelia Müller. 2014. "Ways of Viewing Metaphor in Gesture." In *Body – Language – Communication. An International Handbook on Multimodality in Human Interaction*, edited by Cornelia Müller, Alan Cienki, Ellen Fricke, Silva H. Ladewig, David McNeill, and Jana Bressem, 1766–1780. Berlin/Boston, MA: De Gruyter Mouton.

Clark, Herbert H. 1996. *Using Language*. Cambridge: Cambridge University Press.
Du Bois, John W. 2014. "Towards a Dialogic Syntax." *Cognitive Linguistics* 25 (3): 359–410.
Fillmore, Charles J. 1985. "Frames and the Semantics of Understanding." *Quaderni di Semantica* 6 (2): 222–254.
Fricke, Ellen. 2007. *Origo, Geste und Raum. Lokaldeixis im Deutschen*. Berlin: Walter de Gruyter.
Fricke, Ellen. 2012. *Grammatik multimodal. Wie Wörter und Gesten zusammenwirken*. Berlin: De Gruyter.
Geeraerts, Dirk, and Hubert Cuyckens, eds. 2007. *The Oxford Handbook of Cognitive Linguistics*. New York, NY: Oxford University Press.
Gibbs, Raymond W. Jr. 1994. *The Poetics of Mind. Figurative Thought, Language, and Understanding*. Cambridge: Cambridge University Press.
Harris, Randy A. 1993. *The Linguistics Wars*. New York, NY: Oxford University Press.
Hausman, Carl R. 1989. *Metaphor and Art. Interactionism and Reference in the Verbal and Nonverbal Arts*. Cambridge: Cambridge University Press.
Hostetter, Autumn B., and Martha W. Alibali. 2008. "Visible Embodiment. Gestures as Simulated Action." *Psychonomic Bulletin and Review* 15 (3): 495–514.
Iverson, Jana M., and Esther Thelen. 1999. "Hand, Mouth and Brain. The Dynamic Emergence of Speech and Gesture." *Journal of Consciousness Studies* 6 (11–12): 19–40.
Jakobson, Roman. 1956. "Two Aspects of Language and Two Types of Aphasic Disturbances." In *Fundamentals of Language*, edited by Roman Jakobson and Morris Halle, 53–82. The Hague: Mouton & Co.
Jakobson, Roman. 1960. "Closing Statement. Linguistics and Poetics." In *Style in Language*, edited by Thomas A. Sebeok, 350–449. Cambridge, MA: MIT Press.
Kant, Immanuel. 1902 *Kritik der Urteilskraft. Kants gesammelte Schriften* Vol. 5. Berlin: Walter de Gruyter. Original edition 1790.
Kendon, Adam. 2004. *Gesture. Visible Action as Utterance*. Cambridge: Cambridge University Press.
Kendon, Adam. 2015. "Gesture and Sign. Utterance Uses of Visible Bodily Action." In *The Routledge Handbook of Linguistics*, edited by Keith Allen, 33–46. London: Routledge.
Ladewig, Silva H. 2014. "Creating Multimodal Utterances. The Linear Integration of Gestures into Speech." In *Body – Language – Communication. An International Handbook on Multimodality in Human Interaction*, edited by Cornelia Müller, Alan Cienki, Ellen Fricke, Silva H. Ladewig, David McNeill, and Jana Bressem, 1662–1677. Berlin: De Gruyter Mouton.
Lakoff, George, and Mark Johnson. 1980. *Metaphors We Live By*. Chicago, IL: University of Chicago Press.
Langacker, Ronald W. 1987. *Foundations of Cognitive Grammar* Vol. 1. Stanford, CA: Stanford University Press.
Langacker, Ronald W. 1988. "A Usage-Based Model. Topics in Cognitive Linguistics." In *Topics in Cognitive Linguistics*, edited by Brygida Rudzka-Ostyn, 127–161. Amsterdam: John Benjamins.
Leddy, Thomas. 2012. *The Extraordinary in the Ordinary. The Aesthetics of Everyday Life*. Peterborough: Broadview Press.
Light, Andrew, and Jonathan M. Smith, eds. 2005. *The Aesthetics of Everyday Life*. New York, NY: Columbia University Press.
Linell, Per. 2005. *The Written Language Bias in Linguistics. Its Nature, Origins, and Transformations*. London: Routledge.
Marghetis, Tyler, and Benjamin K. Bergen. 2014. "Embodied Meaning, Inside and Out. The Coupling of Gesture and Mental Simulation." In *Body – Language – Communication. An International Handbook on Multimodality in Human Interaction*, edited by Cornelia Müller,

Alan Cienki, Ellen Fricke, Silva H. Ladewig, David McNeill, and Jana Bressem, 2000–2007. Berlin: De Gruyter Mouton.

McNeill, David, and Elena T. Levy. 1993. "Cohesion and Gesture." *Discourse Processes* 16: 363–386.

McNeill, David, Francis Quek, Karl-Erik McCullough, Susan Duncan, Nobuhiro Furuyama, Robert Bryll, Xin-Feng Ma, and Rashid Ansar. 2001. "Catchments, Prosody and Discourse." *Gesture* 1 (1): 9–33.

Merleau-Ponty, Maurice. 2002. *Phenomenology of Perception*. London: Routledge. Original edition 1945.

Müller, Cornelia. 1998a. "Iconicity and Gesture." In *Oralité et Gestualité: Communication Multimodale, Interaction*, edited by Serge Santi, 321–328. Montréal: L'Harmattan.

Müller, Cornelia. 1998b. *Redebegleitende Gesten. Kulturgeschichte, Theorie, Sprachvergleich*. Berlin: Berlin Verlag Arno Spitz.

Müller, Cornelia. 2010. "Wie Gesten bedeuten. Eine kognitiv-linguistische und sequenzanalytische Perspektive." *Sprache und Gestik. Sonderheft der Zeitschrift Sprache und Literatur* 41 (1): 37–68.

Müller, Cornelia. 2014. "Gestural Modes of Representation as Techniques of Depiction." In *Body – Language – Communication. An International Handbook on Multimodality in Human Interaction*, edited by Cornelia Müller, Alan Cienki, Ellen Fricke, Silva H. Ladewig, David McNeill, and Jana Bressem, 687–1702. Berlin: De Gruyter Mouton.

Müller, Cornelia. 2016. "From Mimesis to Meaning. A Systematics of Gestural Mimesis for Concrete and Abstract Referential Gestures." In *Meaning, Mind and Communication. Explorations in Cognitive Semiotics*, edited by Jordan Zlatev, Göran Sonesson, and Piotr Konderak, 211–226. Frankfurt/M.: Peter Lang.

Müller, Cornelia, and Hermann Kappelhoff. 2018. *Cinematic Metaphor. Experience – Affectivity – Temporality*. In collaboration with Sarah Greifenstein, Dorothea Horst, Thomas Scherer, and Christina Schmitt. Berlin/Boston, MA: Walter de Gruyter.

Rosch, Eleanor, Carolyn B. Mervis, Wayne D. Gray, David M. Johnson, and Penny Boyes-Braem. 1976. "Basic Objects in Natural Categories." *Cognitive Psychology* 8: 382–439.

Saito, Yuriko. 2015. "Aesthetics of the Everyday". In *The Stanford Encyclopedia of Philosophy*, edited by Edward N. Zalta. plato.stanford.edu/archives/win2015/entries/aesthetics-of-everyday. Accessed 26 December 2017.

Schoonjans, Steven. 2014. "Modalpartikeln als multimodale Konstruktionen. Eine korpusbasierte Kookkurrenzanalyse von Modalpartikeln und Gestik im Deutschen." PhD Unpublished Dissertation, Katholieke Universiteit Leuven.

Shklovskiy, Viktor. 1929. *O teorii prozy [On Prose Theory]*. Moscow: Federaciya.

Streeck, Jürgen. 2008. "Depicting by Gestures." *Gesture* 8 (3): 285–301.

Streeck, Jürgen. 2009. *Gesturecraft. The Manu-Facture of Meaning*. Amsterdam: John Benjamins.

Sweetser, Eve. 1998. "Regular Metaphoricity in Gesture. Bodily-based Models of Speech Interaction." Actes du 16e Congrès International des Linguistes (CD-ROM), Elsevier.

Tannen, Deborah. 1989. *Talking Voices. Repetition, Dialogue, and Imagery in Conversational Discourse*. Cambridge: Cambridge University Press.

Tong, Yao. "An Inquiry into Gestures Depicting Concrete and Abstract Concepts." PhD in preparation, Vrije Universiteit.

Turner, Mark. 1996. *The Literary Mind*. New York: Oxford University Press.

Wu, Suwei. "Transitivity, Multimodality and Gesture." PhD in preparation, Vrije Universiteit.

Zima, Elisabeth, and Alexander Bergs. 2017. "Special Issue. Towards a Multimodal Construction Grammar." *Linguistics Vanguard* 3 (s1).

Kathrin Fahlenbrach
Moving Metaphors: Affects, Movements, and Embodied Metaphors in Cinema

Preliminary remarks

A key reason why we enjoy movies lies in the way they attract our feelings, affects, and senses. In their dense creation of images, sounds, and movements, they produce multimodal artefacts which attract us already at a primary level of sensory and even multisensory perception. Experiencing a movie at this level mostly happens without being experienced consciously. Since quite a while, there is a lot of research in film- and media studies dealing with the bodily and affective interplay between viewers and movies. Most notably, phenomenological approaches (e.g. Shaviro 1994, Marks 2000, Sobchack 2004) study the corporal engagement of spectators in viewing and experiencing movies. In addition, several cognitive film and media scholars examine the way films and other moving images address our minds and our senses (e.g. Anderson 1996, Grodal 1997, 2009, Plantinga and Smith 1999).

While both research traditions have a common interest in discovering the difficult to grasp, complex aspects of embodied film viewing, they certainly differ in their approaches and methods. Only one general difference should be mentioned: phenomenological studies, mostly based on philosophy and the arts, tend to avoid general conclusions and programmatically focus on the very specificity in the interaction of single artefacts and viewers; cognitivist studies, primarily based on cognitive psychology, search for recurrent structures in the interplay of films and viewers. While in the first tradition body and affects are treated as dynamic phenomena that cannot be described in a fixed manner, the second tradition is interested in sensory and affective dynamics that result from more or less constant structures both in human perception and in movies (e.g., conventions of styles). Somehow, both traditions look at different sides of one and the same coin: phenomenologists focusing on individual and specific dynamics between moving images and spectators; cognitivists looking at recurrent audiovisual structures of evoking common effects and understandings in viewers. Nonetheless, the two traditions can, in some aspects, enter into a rewarding exchange. And maybe research in embodied metaphorical aesthetics and meanings of moving images is especially convenient for broadening the scope on both sides, as it is always confronted by metaphors with rather fuzzy and affectively loaded meanings, which are very difficult to generalize.

https://doi.org/10.1515/9783110615036-005

This paper, along with this volume, takes up the interdisciplinary and inter discursive exchange initiated by the Center for Advanced Film Studies *Cinepoetics*. Starting with a reading of papers on 'cinematic expressive movements' and metaphors by Kappelhoff, Müller, and colleagues, I will then present a cognitivist approach to audiovisual metaphors and embodied meanings in moving images. With a case study of RUN LOLA RUN [LOLA RENNT] (Tom Tykwer, GER 1998) I will demonstrate the compatibility of both approaches as well as their specific differences.

Cinematic expressive movements and metaphors: A cognitive reading and some questions

In their *Cinematic Metaphor* approach, Hermann Kappelhoff and Cornelia Müller, together with Sarah Greifenstein, Dorothea Horst, Thomas Scherer, and Christina Schmitt, combine a phenomenological interest in multifaceted, fluid, embodied and affective phenomena in cinematic aesthetics (or rather: *aisthesis*) with a more structural goal of investigating the general dynamics between spectator and moving images. While focusing on the subjectivity and specificity of aesthetic/ *aisthestic* experiences, they offer a new perspective within phenomenological film and media studies, including cognitive research on gestures (e.g. Cienki and Müller 2008, Müller 2008). One of their basic assumptions is that we interact with movies via our senses and our affects in a similar way as we do in interpersonal communication with others. More specifically, they argue that gestures and other forms of embodied communication create intersubjective expressions, emerging from the specific bodily and affective interaction and dynamics between the people involved:

> Gestures are intersubjective acts of expression and perception. Thus, we perceive of them as direct, unmediated expression, and we think of interaffectivity, rather than of affect expression of an individual speaker. (Müller and Kappelhoff 2018, 148)

Gestures not only communicate the inner affects of one person, but also express the dyadic or collective dynamics between persons in an interaction. As such, gestures are taken as a key medium for interaffectivity. As Müller and Kappelhoff argue, they are performed in multimodal gestalts in which it is not only the gestural forming of the hand that is creating the gestalt. It is also formed by the movement patterns of the hand, the tempo and rhythm of the movements, and, furthermore, the way they are orchestrated by other bodily expressive modes (e.g., body posture, facial expression, gazes, movements of the head), by the voice, and by spoken words. As a result, gestures are considered here as key elements in holistic, multimodal processes of interpersonal and interaffective communication, and as such are an elementary mode of human communication. Taking this awareness into account, Kappelhoff, Müller, and colleagues assume a similar dynamic between moving images and their spectators. Here the temporal dimension of gestures and moving images, as well as the patterns and gestalts of movements in different modi, are taken as a significant analogy. More specifically, they consider moving images as expressive movements, similar to human gestures in that they express the affective and bodily interaction with spectators in a multimodal way, summarizing:

> Against such a theoretical frame, the film image is regarded in a similar way to a facial expression or an unfolding hand gesture in its temporal dynamics. This, and we have mentioned it already, includes all levels of the shaping of the film image as elements of a dynamic figuration of expression: acting but also color, lighting, set design, music, montage, etc. (Müller and Kappelhoff 2018, 163)

This general analogy between the aesthetics of moving images and gestural expression in human communication is further specified by drawing on metaphorical gestures. As Müller (2008) and others (e.g., Cienki and Müller 2008, Cienki this volume) have shown in their works, gestures can generate in human interactions metaphorical gestalts and meanings. The gestalt of metaphorical gestures, again, emerges from the very interactive dynamics and the interplay of different modes of expression. While all phenomenal elements of bodily expressions are taken as significant forms of an interaction, metaphors are special in their embodied conciseness. The form of the hands, movement patterns etc., are performed in a way that refers to other experiential domains, thereby expressing an idea, feeling, or affect in an experientially based image. As Müller (2008) showed, an image performed by a gesture can act as a metaphorical source for the spoken words to follow. For *Cinematic Metaphor*, these insights are related to the study of cinematic aesthetics:

> [...], we have then argued that expressive movements modulate affective experiences in an immediate process of perceiving and that, in this process, metaphorical meaning emerges that is 'experientially based' in the most literal sense of the word. (Müller and Kappelhoff 2018, 178)

This programmatically implies a non-representational account of moving images, assuming that representations are solely created within the process of film viewing:

> Visual representations are not already given with the image but are themselves the result of complex processes of fictionalization. For any understanding of what is represented in the image, the audiovisual data of the moving film image must above all already be realized as the embodied experience of the senses. (Kappelhoff and Greifenstein 2016, 184)

This argument also implies that moving images do not represent conceptual knowledge to be initiated in viewers. Instead, it is presumed that viewers construct original cinematic meanings from their specific interactions with given moving images. Accordingly, two aspects of cinematic metaphors can be observed which seem to be closely related. On the one hand, metaphors are taken as a general mode of fictionalization during film reception. As Kappelhoff and Greifenstein argue:

> From this perspective, spectators themselves let moving images become visual representations in the modes of metaphor-making of "seeing one thing in terms of another" (Müller 2008, 26–32) and these representations indicate an artistically created, manufactured, fictional world in their every trait. [...] This is the sense in which we understand the reception of film images as poiesis, as an act of artistic production, which is to be found in media consumption itself (Certeau 1984). (Kappelhoff and Greifenstein 2016, 184)

In other words, the very nature of film experience is regarded as being genuinely metaphoric. Film reception, "the expression of experience by experience" (Sobchack 1992), is then generally taken as the metaphorical transfer of a cinematically expressed experience into the experience of a spectator, 'as if' it was her own. On the other hand, cinematic metaphors are considered as gradually unfolding and specific meaning-making processes during film viewing. Accordingly, conceptual meanings are only generated in film viewing, feeding from affectively and bodily experienced expressions and gestalts that act as sources for higher meanings. In their analysis of the movie JEZEBEL (William Wyler, USA 1938) Kappelhoff and Müller (2011, see also Müller and Kappelhoff 2018) demonstrate how cinematic expressive movements within one sequence evolve as a ground for metaphorical meaning around the performance of the character Julie: dynamic, expansive, powerful movements become straight and focused, then turn into a continuous flow of slower movements when she enters a rather static environment, turning into a dance-like performance within this immobile group of people until they are finally stopped. Kappelhoff and Müller (2011, 145), in their detailed reconstruction of the dynamic shapes in Julie's movements and their cinematic staging, find a key metaphor of the movie: *the society is experienced and understood as a static structure with a dynamic force in it.*

Given the saliency of the staged movements' patterns and their bodily and affective impact, it seems evident and convincing that this is a metaphorical meaning which might arise in most viewers by their very sensory and affective experience of the sequence. The analysis of Kappelhoff and Müller points to the connections the film is drawing between Julie's dynamic movements, her wild horse, and black people serving white people, which equally highlight the immobility of the white social majority there. This embodied metaphorical meaning is then elaborated for a more conceptually based interpretation, that "the experience of being slowed down or dropped combines with the expression of being suppressed as a woman", or "excluded from society as a slave".

This detailed analysis of the cinematic expressive movements is fully convincing. However, some methodological questions arise regarding the emergence of conceptual meanings in metaphorical shapes. The specific social meanings being attributed to the different persons and groups as representatives for 'a socially unconventional person' (dynamic Julie), 'the white society' (the static group of white guests), and 'slaves' (black people serving them) seem to be implicitly related to their stereotypical representations in clothing and habits. Yet these correlations are not explained explicitly. Also, this would contrast the non-representational account of the authors. Rather it is assumed that such conceptual meanings on social understandings of the staged situations are evolving from the very bodily and affective experience of viewers. As Kappelhoff and Müller conclude more generally:

> [...] a world arises that is characterized by the opposition between a static society, which creates and allocates positions – like master, servant, man, women, slave, citizen – and movements of the slaves who keep this society alive. (Kappelhoff and Müller 2011, 147)

Yet how, within the dense composition of expressive movement patterns, are such specific social roles, structures and even their critique evoked in viewers? And how does such a complex and abstract concept as 'society' come into play? Since the cognitive salience of social schemas and stereotypes in film viewing is rather negated by Kappelhoff, Müller and colleagues (e.g. Schmitt, Greifenstein, and Kappelhoff 2014), together with a representational perspective, there seems to be a gap between the rich and convincing analyses of cinematic expressive movements, related with basic embodied metaphorical meanings, and the identification of cinematic metaphors, including abstract and conceptually-based meanings. Since this affects the question of metaphorical targets on the level of higher semantics, it would be important to know more about how conceptual knowledge is involved in those metaphorical processes which go beyond a purely bodily and affective experience (e.g., of static vs. dynamic movements in its different shapes). While *Cinematic Metaphor* considerably contributes to a more distinguished understanding of embodied aesthetics and experience of film, its understanding of how abstract meanings emerge in these dynamic processes remains rather opaque. In her works on metaphorical gestures, Müller (e.g., 2008) refers to spoken language as a relevant source for conceptual understanding and bringing experience into play. Maybe, it might be helpful to look more specifically for the equivalents of spoken language and their semantics in the experience and understanding of moving images.

The next section will present a cognitive approach to audiovisual metaphors in moving images that also takes embodied experiences as a key source for metaphorical meanings and their experience by viewers. While both approaches differ in some general epistemological and methodological respects, I will take the opportunity of this volume to take up some of the ideas of Kappelhoff, Müller, and colleagues, and further elaborate assumptions on motion-based, interaffective qualities of metaphorical meanings in moving images.

Audiovisual metaphors: A cognitive approach to embodied cinematic meanings

Some general assumptions of cognitive film and media theory

There are two general assumptions in cognitive film and media studies which heavily influence their understanding of metaphors in moving images. First, and in contrast to phenomenological ideas, films and other media are taken as representations of meanings, shaped by artists and producers of audiovisual artifacts. It is presumed that especially popular audiovisual media (movies, TV shows, video games etc.) are designed with the intention to reach a broad audience by creating artifacts that attract them sensorially, affectively, and cognitively (Anderson 1996, Anderson and Fisher Anderson 2005, Grodal 1997, 2009, Plantinga and Smith 1999, Nannicelli and Taberham 2014). Accordingly, moving images perform sensorially rich audio-visions, tell compelling stories, and offer views, appraisals, and interpretations of the world. This assumption is epistemologically supported by the anthropological observation that storytelling lies at the very roots of human culture, and even psychophysical disposition (e.g. Turner 1996, Boyd 2009). Accordingly, humans have always created stories to understand the world. From a psychological viewpoint, though, humans always seek for a cognitive coherence to their surrounding world and their being there. They are continuously making sense of what they perceive – and what they perceive is already reflexively categorized by the activation of cognitive schemas (Anderson 2005, Johnson 1987, Lakoff 1987). When viewing moving images, primary processes of mental and cognitive categorization are initiated by everything that is audiovisually presented, even in an unconscious manner. At the same time, psychology teaches us that we are of course not just cognitive beings but are also in a constant exchange with our environment via all our senses, organs, and by our affects. As psychologist Bruce Goldstein (2010) explains, we are constantly interacting psycho-physically with our surroundings. In ongoing circular processes, we permanently relate the multisensory and affective experiences of stimuli, conceptual knowledge, memory and body actions (Goldstein 2010, 5ff). Returning to audiovisual media, they somehow offer us analogues for these vital circular processes. Audiovisual media permit viewers multimodal experiences which draw on bodily and affectively, but also cognitively, anchored human ways of experiencing oneself in the world and making sense of it.

Second, cognitive film and media scholars tend to search for those recurring experiential structures and represented meanings of moving images that are designed to be felt and understood by a majority of the audience. This implies, on the one hand, a semiotic requirement of codes and conventions in genres and styles that act as communicative interfaces between producers and recipients. On the other hand, analyzing such recurrent experiential and semantic structures affords the opportunity to generalize the possible experiences, feelings and understandings of viewers by drawing on psychological insights on human perception and cognition, as well as on media effects. As David Bordwell (1987) put it, cognitive film- and media scholars start from 'idealized models' of viewers, built on empirical knowledge about human mind and psyche. This not only concerns conceptual knowledge but also the exploration of the embodied, pre-conceptual dimension of audiovisual media and its reception. As mentioned at the beginning, significant research has been done in cognitive film and media studies to study reflexively and affectively-anchored aspects in the viewing of moving images – especially by ecological and evolutionary based approaches (Anderson 1996, Grodal 1997, 2009). Also, cognitive approaches to cinematic or audiovisual metaphors in moving images study recurrent embodied dimensions as pre-conceptual and affectively-based sources for the performance of more abstract or complex meanings. As I will outline in the next paragraphs, different gestalt-based sources stand at the fore of cognitive metaphor accounts, which are manifest in each audiovisual composition of images, sounds, and movements. This opens the ground for more specific considerations of the dynamic and fluid meaning structures of audiovisual meanings.

Gestalt perception as a source for audiovisual metaphors: textures, surfaces, and body shapes

At a basic level, cognitive approaches to metaphors (e.g. Forceville 2011, 2017, Forceville and Jeulink 2011, Fahlenbrach 2007, 2008, 2010, 2016b, 2017a, Urios-Aparisi 2010, Coëgnarts and Kravanja 2012, 2014) in moving images start from a similar presumption as Kappelhoff, Müller, and colleagues: metaphors in moving images are anchored in embodied experiences that might be evoked in viewers by the audiovisual composition of images, sounds, and movements. Furthermore, in line with cognitive assumptions mentioned before, it is further assumed that metaphors are intentionally created by producers of audiovisual artifacts in order to guide viewer's experience and understanding in a way based on generalized hypotheses of an idealized viewer. As I argue in my approach to audiovisual metaphors (e.g. 2016a), one of the main functions of metaphors in moving images is to create deictic structures that let viewers experience key meanings of a narrative (be it entertaining or informing) already bodily and affectively, and mostly before becoming aware of it. This implies that our semantic understanding already starts at a low level of mental perception and affective appraisal. Audiovisual metaphors in movies, TV shows, news, or video games draw on physically-rooted mechanisms of mental perception that allow for reflexive bodily and affective responses and mental recognition. As cognitive psychology has shown, this is based on our general capacity of gestalt perception that is anchored in our brains (Goldstein 2010) and that creates gestalt patterns of multimodal stimuli that help us to quickly make sense of what we perceive, even unconsciously. This includes vital affective appraisals. Round, square, soft, sharp, big or small shapes for example are affectively appraised specifically, and hence evoke different ways of experiencing them (e.g., pleasant, unpleasant, defensive or offensive). Audiovisual media, notably entertaining movies and video games, create textures, surfaces, body shapes of characters and objects that directly address our gestalt perception and evoke multisensory associations that go widely beyond audiovisual perception. Sound, in particular, is used to widen viewer's sensory associations towards tactile and sensory-motor ones. These can be designed in a metaphorical way to combine bodily, affective experiences of a moving image with more abstract semantics of a narrative.

An example would be a sequence from STAR WARS. EPISODE II (George Lucas, USA 2002) (Fahlenbrach 2010, 152ff). In this sequence ('The Battle of Geonosis') the protagonists Obi-Wan Kenobi, Anakin Skywalker, and Princess Padme are condemned on a hostile planet to being executed in a huge arena by three monster-like beings. The Acklay, one of these, has a huge and voluminous body with scissor-like legs that move in a chaotic way, a head with a big toothed mouth, and a prickly and puckered skin. Its body shape combines the appearances of a dinosaur, a crab, and a mantis. As the production designer of this figure Robert Barnes comments: "The Acklay was for me the embodiment of chaos" (in Vaz 2002, 145). With its surface and texture, the wrinkles, fissures, claws, and flapper-like organs that are distributed on its body in an irregular way, it is designed to reflexively evoke discomfort. This being is intensified acoustically by its high buzzing roars and the sharp sounds of its scissor-like legs on the ground, which evoke intensively negative tactile associations and affects. On a basic gestalt level, its perception is anchored in its chaotic, dissonant appearance, creating disorientation, loss of control and discomfort in viewers. Disorientation being mentally reinforced by merging attributes of different animals and beings. As such, production design and cinematography here create a fictional being with an audiovisual body that viewers can recognize and experience reflexively as being 'dangerous', 'offensive', and 'disgusting'. Within the context of the movie, and more specifically of this sequence, its chaotic body gestalt generates a metaphorical meaning. Being part of the antagonistic forces that the protagonists combat in the film, a more abstract and conceptual meaning comes into play related to the narrative and that makes it not only dangerous and hostile, but – in a metaphorical way – also 'evil'. Hence all the specific attributes of its bodily appearance, its surfaces, textures and its performance, are shaped to be experienced by viewers already reflexively as qualities of an 'evil being'.

Embodied image schemas as sources for audiovisual metaphors

Another embodied level of semantic experience and understanding that is of key relevance for metaphorical displays are image schemas. In cognitive linguistics image schemas are understood as mental patterns resulting from vital and omnipresent bodily experiences. As Johnson puts it: "An image schema is a recurring, dynamic pattern of our perceptual interactions and motor programs that gives coherence to our experience" (Johnson 1987, xiv). More specifically, they derive from our movements and interactions, including different parts of the body, sometimes all of them (cf. also Gibbs 2006). Most notably, the *force*-schema originates from the fact that in every action and interaction we are regularly exerting force on our surroundings while at the same time (e. g. physical, mechanical, bodily or other natural) forces are exerted upon us (e.g., gravity, wind, handshakes). The *container*-schema emerges from the vital and omnipresent experience of our bodies as entities with external limits that we are keen to protect, e.g., by wearing clothes and building houses as external containers. Other image schemas relate to the embodied experience of *balance* or of orienting and moving in spaces by *paths*.

Image schemas imply multisensory experiential qualities because the whole body and all senses are concerned. As dynamic patterns, they do not only appear in a fixed form. Rather they obtain some key gestalt qualities that can be experienced in very different shapes. As Johnson (1987, 43ff) explains it for the force schema: forces always have a directionality, resulting from the interaction between two or more agents executing force on each other (e.g., the heavy rain as a natural force, falling from above). Forces also imply grades of intensity (e.g., strong-weak).

More specifically, interactions of agents create different gestalts of forces with concrete expressive elements, such as *compulsion* (dominant force of one agent exerted onto another), *blockage* (executed force of one agent being repulsed), *counterforce* (interaction between forces of two agents), or *attraction* (one agent being moved to another one). Gestalt elements of other image schemas are for instance: in-out, closed-open, big-small (*container*) or source-path-goal, straight-devious (*paths*). Obviously, image schemas have embodied gestalts that make them significant; however, these can manifest at the same time in different forms and appearances. Based on gestalt perception, they also guide in a relevant way our conceptual understanding of situations on a reflexive level that is mostly unnoticed. As Johnson notes on image schemas:

> [...] I shall emphasize their gestalt characteristics, that is, their nature as coherent, meaningful, unified wholes within our experience and cognition. They are principle means by which we achieve meaning structure. [...] Most important, these "experiential gestalts" are neither arbitrary, nor are they "mushy" forms that have no internal structure. (Johnson 1987, 41)

As has been argued by Lakoff (1987), Johnson (1987), Kövecses (2003), Gibbs (2006), and others, image schemas are a relevant source in metaphorical meaning making processes. These dynamic, multisensory patterns with significant gestalt elements offer a broad spectrum of giving shape to more abstract, conceptual meanings. More specifically, embodied image schemas are activated in order to project them onto a concept which is more difficult to grasp and is part of a different experiential domain (e.g., 'society' or 'love'). By projecting the gestalt structure (e.g., in-out) of an embodied source domain (e.g., 'building': container) onto the semantic structure of the target domain (e.g., society), a third, metaphorical meaning is created (e.g., SOCIETY IS A HOUSE, enabling us for example to talk of 'entering a society') (Fahlenbrach 2016a).

As has been shown (e.g. Forceville 2011, 2017, Forceville and Jeulink 2011, Fahlenbrach 2007, 2008, 2010, 2016b, 2017a, b, Urios-Aparisi 2010, Coëgnarts and Kravanja 2012, 2014), moving images make abundant use of image schemas as sources for metaphorical displays. As such, they are addressed in moving images by pictures, sounds, and movements to trigger specific and rich conceptual meanings that are related with an experiential flow of associations and affects (Fahlenbrach 2016b). Movies, television shows, video games, or other moving images repeatedly generate audiovisual metaphors in their motifs and in their audiovisual compositions a) by manifesting conceptual metaphors already established in our minds and in (media-)culture; and b) by creating original mappings in the metaphorical use of embodied source domains (e.g., image schemas). These are elements of the very audiovisual composition, and abstract or complex target domains in the genre-typical semantic framework of a piece. I understand audiovisual metaphors as intentionally created symbolic forms and relevant elements in audiovisual media (Fahlenbrach 2010, 2016a). Audiovisual metaphors transfer cultural meanings in mentally and bodily rooted metaphorical gestalts. To do this, they use salient gestalt patterns in image, sound, and movement that are closely related to embodied image schemas in our minds as metaphorical source domains. Audiovisual metaphors thereby generate cross-modal mappings across different domains. They address multi-sensorial qualities of the related image schemas, which are manifested in the visual composition, sound design, music, and movements.

Affective cross-modal gestalts as embodied sources for audiovisual metaphors

The multisensory aesthetics of audiovisual metaphors and their experience is significantly anchored in cross-modal perception, which is the integration of divergent stimuli by amodal qualities (Fahlenbrach 2008, 2010). Psychologically, we can mentally unite cross-modal gestalts by processing stimuli received by different senses in terms of their *intensity, duration, rhythm*, or *position* – qualities that can be processed by all senses. As psychologist Daniel Stern (1985, 1999) has shown, our natural disposition for cross-modal perception is a relevant precondition for affective interactions. More specifically, humans interact to a considerable degree at the level of *vitality affects*: non-categorical affects (distinct from categorical and causal emotions) that continuously accompany our existence (cf. Koppe, Harder, and Vaever 2008). They are related with vital somatic and mental processes like breathing, sleeping, or just 'being' in any kind of bodily and mental activity. Vitality affects not only have an inner experiential dimension, but also a performative one of "activating contours" (Koppe, Harder, and Vaever 2008, 170). These are embodied and affective gestalts that might be experienced and performed cross-modally by including the whole body (mimics, gestures, voice, movements etc.). Significantly enough, and given their experiential complexity, they tend to be described and conceptualized by metaphors, such as: "surging", "fading away", "fleeting", "exploding" or "bursting". Following Stern (1999, 68), interpersonal interactions always imply vital affective attunement by cross-modal contours or gestalts, emerging from our bodily behavior in an interaction. Similar to what Müller (e.g., 2008) observed for co-verbal gestures, the cross-modal gestalts or contours highly depend on the interaffective dynamics in an interaction and might result in affective dyads (or collectives). They share vitality affects by dynamically generating affective contours in their embodied interactions. Both Müller and Stern consider affective gestalts or contours as temporal and movement based. For metaphorical performances in moving images this implies, as I would argue, at least three aspects: first, moving images can – as Kappelhoff, Müller, and colleagues argue – evoke affective attunement with viewers ("cinematic expressive movements") by all means of cinematic forms that generate metaphorical gestalts (e.g. 'bursting' or 'fading'). Second – and from a more cognitive stance – the metaphorical gestalts of affective contours which we know from our everyday interaction and bodily being are represented in audiovisual performances. This is especially relevant in depicting affective interactions of characters on the screen for a broad audience. And third, these affective gestalts are used as source domains for creating more abstract metaphorical meanings in moving images.

The highly aesthetic creation of such metaphorical performances generates audiovisual gestalts by referring to principles of cross-modal perception. The cross-modal interaction of pictures and sound lets viewers integrate visual and acoustic information to coherent gestalts and meanings, based on the processing of amodal qualities such as *duration* (long-short), *intensity* (strong-weak), and *position* (above-below, central-peripheral, close-distant). As I proposed elsewhere (e.g. 2008, 2010, 2017b), this cross-modal aesthetic can imply the following forms:
- *Cross-modal duration and rhythm*: duration (long vs. short) and rhythm (quick vs. slow) of shots and their temporal succession within the editing; the duration of the depicted movements in pictures and of the camera movements might interact cross-modally with the acoustic duration and tempo of sounds and music.
- *Cross-modal intensity*: visual and auditory elements in a cinematic sequence interrelate in their density of sensory stimuli, resulting in specific cross-modal intensities (strong vs. weak); on the visual scale the intensity of colors (e.g. intensity of color saturation or intensity of color contrasts) and of lighting (intensity of brightness vs. intensity of darkness) interacts on the auditory scale with the intensity of acoustic volume (loud vs. calm) and the pitch (intensity of high vs. low pitch) in music and sounds.
- *Cross-modal position*: visual closeness or distance in camera shots and perspective, as well as spatial foreground and background in the picture interact with acoustic closeness or distance as well as acoustic foreground and background. These can be established e.g. by the acoustic perspective (point-of-audition, Chion 1994) of characters in the foreground or background of a filmic space and by providing an acoustic perspective in the balancing of volume between loud (foreground) and low (background).

It is by relating images and sounds in terms of amodal qualities that they merge not only into audiovisual units, what Michel Chion (1994) calls *synchresis*. Furthermore, they might evoke bodily and mental associations based on much more senses, such as tactile, sensory-motor, or even olfactory ones. Such cross-modal gestalts, rooted in our omnipresent experience of vitality affects, offer rich embodied and affective sources for audiovisual metaphors.

Having sketched some general principles of gestalt perception, embodied image schemas, and affective gestalt contours as sources for audiovisual metaphors, I will offer an example of my approach in a case study.

Case study: RUN LOLA RUN

In order to strengthen the dialog between phenomenological and cognitive approaches, I chose for my case study a film that has also been used by Müller and Kappelhoff (2018) to demonstrate principles of cinematic expressive movements: Tom Tykwer's RUN LOLA RUN [LOLA RENNT] (GER 1998). The movie tells the story of Lola (Franka Potente), who has twenty minutes to help her boyfriend Manni (Moritz Bleibtreu) obtain 100.000 Deutsche Mark (former German currency) which he owes to some criminals and he has just lost in the subway – Lola runs across Berlin to help Manni out of this serious problem. The film is indeed a very telling example for the possibilities of movies to create different layers of embodied and affective expressions by the shaping of images, sounds, and movements. Müller and Kappelhoff focus on a sequence just before Lola starts her run. In their detailed analysis of the sequence where Manni, fearing for his life, explains to Lola his desperate situation on the phone, they show the specific "orchestration" of movement by different cinematic forms and its resulting affective expression. Their analysis concludes:

> What goes along with this aesthetic orchestration of cinematic movement is an affective flow moving from horror to increasing stress, that is modulated through the montage movement and through the changing of movement qualities: a slow and calm movement is interrupted harshly by a keen and fast staccato of repeated perspectives and voices, culminating in an increasing and extended loud and shrill sound staging. This composition of movement-images is what affects the viewers. It is the temporal orchestration of the cinematic movement gestalt that is experienced as an immediate affectivity by viewers. (Müller and Kappelhoff 2018, 133)

Obviously, the sequence creates dynamic gestalt patterns, akin to affective contours, that let emerge expressive cinematic experiences. In my analysis of the 'first run', I will show that this is equally true for the following parts of the movie. As I will show, such expressive gestalts are also used to shape metaphorical meanings of an abstract concept, which is *time*. Because the movie deals with some basic epistemological aspects related to the relativity of time: the distinction between the subjective experience of time, its objective measurement, and the opaqueness of temporal chains of events and their contingency.

Already during the opening credits, viewers are cognitively primed for a cinematic treatment of time: we hear loud ticking sounds and see a huge clock pendulum moving in slow but constant swings, accompanied by a deep and voluminous rumble. The camera moves from below to the top of the clock. There, an archaic monster figure shows up as decorative part of the clock that, by the approach of the camera, opens its mouth and lets the camera move into a black hole. Hence from the beginning, the abstract concept of time is metaphorically performed as a PHYSICAL FORCE, and even a SWALLOWING PHYSICAL FORCE. (Figure 1)

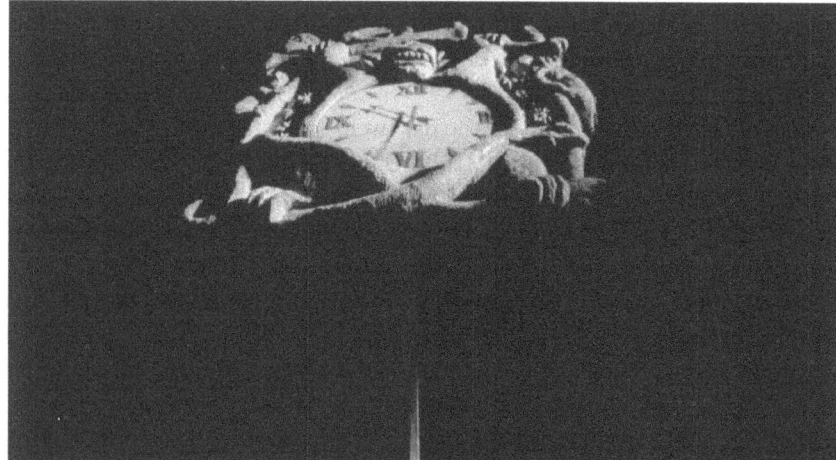

Figure 1: Clock-motif in the front credits: TIME IS A PHYSICAL FORCE (RUN LOLA RUN).

Through the film Manni is predominantly stuck in the same place. Mostly, we see him in the phone booth, desperately trying to find someone to lend him the money. The phone booth is placed in front of a supermarket that Manni wants to hijack if Lola does not appear in time. Standing in the phone box, he regularly looks to a big clock in the building across the street, seeing how time is passing. On the facade of the supermarket, there is a decorative disc with a graphic spiral, continuously moving. Most shots of Manni in the phone booth show the spiral behind him. Its constantly circling rhythm optically reinforces the 'objective' temporal flow that Manni cannot influence. The moving hands of the watch, the moving spiral, together with the ongoing, staccato beats of the film score create a cross-modal impression of 'time as a constantly forward moving force' that Manni is subject to. His static, passive situation is spatially made evident by his placement in the phone booth, a small container that physically limits his action radius. (Figure 2)

Figure 2: Manni in the phone booth (RUN LOLA RUN).

This is strongly contrasted with his desperate and angry expressions. Several shots show him, sometimes from above, loudly yelling into the phone and brutally punching the machine. Accordingly, acting and cinematography create the affective contour of a container with an 'exploding' physical force in it. In the context of the movie, this does not only create the canonical emotion metaphor 'anger is a physical force in a container' (Kövecses 2003), but also relates to the metaphorical display of 'time as physical force' throughout the whole film. Showing Manni visually framed between the clock and spiral, as well as acoustically by the pushing beat of the film score, viewers are invited to experience his situation as being TRAPPED BY TIME AS A CONSTANTLY FORWARD MOVING PHYSICAL FORCE (Figure 3).

Figure 3: Manni 'trapped by time' (RUN LOLA RUN).

The sequences with Manni waiting immobile and 'trapped' at one place are strongly contrasted by the dominating sequences showing Lola's search for help while running through the city. From the beginning, Lola is established as a strong physical force, offensively facing the quick passing of time. In her initial conversation with Manni, Lola loudly screams into the phone at an extremely high pitch. This breaks some glass bottles in her room, and she gives Manni the order: "Stay where you are! In 20 minutes – I'll figure something out […]". The movie then shows us three versions of her attempts to save Manni. Having established from the beginning 'time as a physical force', her rescue efforts are metaphorically performed as bodily confrontations with this force, omnipresent in images and sounds. Throughout the whole movie Lola running through the city is a metaphorical leitmotiv (cf. Fahlenbrach 2016a). Through the interaction of physical actions, camera, editing, and music, this leitmotiv has the concise cross-modal gestalt of a strong bodily force, continually and quickly moving forward, that sometimes is interrupted, blocked or confronted with other force agents. The camera follows her from behind, from ahead and in parallel to her run on lateral camera tracks. During Lola's running sequences, the moving camera mostly adapts the tempo of her body movements. This all supports the gestalt impression of her as a dynamic force, but also offers viewers experiential cues to mentally mirror vital physical qualities of her run (as intense body tension, heavy breathing, determined and fast moves forward).

The staccato beats of the music contribute significantly to an even more cross-modal and affective gestalt of running Lola. The music establishes a specific temporal structure by its tempo, rhythm and succession of instrumental and vocal elements. As an autonomous element, it appears throughout the movie, including the sequences with Manni. Accordingly, as mentioned before, it gives an embodied impression of the continuous and fast time flow of the 20 minutes that both Manni and Lola are confronted with. Hence the key metaphor TIME IS A PHYSICAL FORCE is shaped more specifically by the film score by 'movements in sound', in the concrete gestalts of quick and pushing auditory rhythms and tempi. While Manni, through his immobility, is in a dramatic sense helpless when facing this power, running Lola is presented as offensively adapting to it. Her determined and goal-driven attitude is visually reinforced by the fact that, having once left the circular staircase of her home, she is mostly shown running along straight paths (streets and bridges). (Figure 4)

As a result, in the running-sequences the tempo and rhythm of Lola's movements, of the camera, the editing, and the music merge to create cross-modal gestalts of a dynamic force resolutely moving forward along linear paths, with its movements being synchronous to the tempo and rhythm of the omnipresent, reigning temporal flow of the music.

Aside from the music, the camera also establishes an autonomous temporal structure that is independent from Lola's and Manni's conflict. Although the camera mostly accompanies Lola, it also deviates from her paths, showing other characters with their specific temporal rhythms and conflicts. At the start of her run, the camera leaves her in the apartment and moves into the living room where her mother is chatting in a relaxed manner on the phone, fully ignorant of the dramatic conflict of her daughter (which is at that moment only present by the ongoing music beat). As in some other moments in the film, the camera circles around the figure, creating the gestalt of a person resting immobile within the established time flow. Furthermore, inserts of her father, whom Lola first considers as savior of Manni, and who has a serious talk at the bank office with his lover, establish a contrasting temporal dynamic to that of Lola and Manni: the film music stops,

Figure 4: Lola as a DYNAMIC FORCE running along PATHS (RUN LOLA RUN).

and we see the couple talking silently and slowly to each other. The noticeable way in which the camera diverges in such moments from the temporal order of the protagonists autonomously creates different temporal structures throughout the movie. This specifically feeds into the metaphorical network presented so far: TIME IS MOVEMENT IN SPACE. Similarly to the film score, the movements of the camera offer viewers a bodily concrete impression of time as an invisible force that is, in addition, always experienced subjectively.

In other moments, the camera transports Lola's confrontations with other persons on her run – different in all three versions. In the first version of her run these are for example: a woman with a baby buggy who passes her way and whom she nearly crashes into; a young cyclist who accompanies her for a moment, offering her his bike; a group of nuns who are directly approaching her; and a car driver who crosses her way in a 90–degree angle when slowly leaving a tunnel, narrowly evading a confrontation with her, just before another car fully crashes into his. (Figure 5)

These confrontations result in specific embodied lines of forces. The first confrontation generates a moment of *blockage*, when Lola races against the woman and staggers for a second before continuing her run; the camera, leaving her, stays with the woman and shows her furiously insulting and yelling after her, presenting her as an affective agent. While the leading music continues, the editing then inserts in fast succession a row of photos of the woman's life, acoustically accompanied by the loud clicking sounds of a camera. Again, cinematography creates an audiovisual rhythm and tempo that supports the cross-modal impression that time is movement in sound (music) and space (camera, body movements) and hence generates very different dynamic gestalts, such as slowing down (blockage of Lola) or speeding up (fast tracking of the woman's life). The confrontations with the other people result in force lines like *attraction* (the cyclist approaching her in a focused way), *embracing* (the nuns dividing their group to let her pass in between) or *counterforce* (car crash). Again, the editing inserts for some of them a fast-track sequence of their (future) lives, establishing them not only as bodily but also affective agents on Lola's path.

As a result, different temporal agents are created, both within the pictures, and by camera, editing, music and sounds that let viewers experience different intensities, rhythms and affective gestalts of time flows. In accordance with Müller and Kappelhoff (2018), I would suggest that the movie creates cinematic expressive movements that viewers experience with their bodies and affects, and that generate from their direct interaction with the moving images on the screen. This, as my analysis has shown, further implies a metaphorical performance of time – both as an abstract concept and as an embodied experience. Finally, the noticeable way in which cinematography establishes itself as an autonomous temporal agent also serves to make the film a metaphorical treatment of moving images as a temporal art.

Figure 5: Lines of forces on Lola's run: blockage, embracing, attraction, counterforce (RUN LOLA RUN).

Concluding remarks

As the case study has shown, movies – like other moving images – have a huge potential to give abstract and complex meanings concrete sensory gestalts through their cinematic use of images, sounds, and movements. As is the case for all visual media, movies are widely based on non-propositional forms of expression. Hence audiovisual metaphors are a significant and even elementary way of performing conceptual and abstract meanings.

It has also become evident that the study of embodied metaphors presents a rewarding place to analyze the interface between phenomenological and cognitivist research of moving images. As both traditions are exploring different sides of embodied aesthetics and meanings in audiovisual media, it is particularly through their common study of embodied metaphorical sources like image schemas, affective gestalts or other gestalt patterns that their works can be related in a productive way. While their specific interests might and even should further differ, their exchange can enhance both traditions. Phenomenologists, for instance, might consider the *reflexive* qualities of conceptual schemas which could help to explain how abstract meanings are generated in embodied metaphorical processes. Cognitivists might be more sensitive to the specific embodied and affective gestalt patterns which moving images create and that significantly characterize cinematic aesthetics and their experience. – Hopefully the productive exchange between the two discourses, put forward by *Cinepoetics*, will be continued.

Audiovisual sources

JEZEBEL, Dir. William Wyler. Warner Bros., USA 1938.
RUN LOLA RUN [LOLA RENNT], Dir. Tom Tykwer. X-Filme, GER 1998.
STAR WARS: EPISODE II – ATTACK OF THE CLONES. Dir. George Lucas. 20th Century Fox, USA 2002.

Bibliography

Anderson, John R. 2005. *Cognitive Psychology and Its Implications*. New York: Macmillan.
Anderson, Joseph D. 1996. *The Reality of Illusion. An Ecological Approach to Cognitive Film Theory*. Carbondale, IL: Southern Illinois University Press.
Anderson, Joseph D., and Barbara Fisher Anderson. 2005. *Moving Image Theory. Ecological Considerations*. Carbondale, IL: Southern Illinois University Press.

Bordwell, David. 1987. *Narration in Fiction Film*. London: Routledge.
Boyd, Brian. 2009. *On the Origin of Stories. Evolution, Cognition, and Fiction*. Harvard: Harvard University Press.
Certeau, Michel de. 1984. *The Practice of Everyday Life*. Translated by Steven Rendall. Berkely, CA: University of California Press. Original edition 1980.
Chion, Michel. 1994. *Audio-Vision. Sound on Screen*. New York, NY: Columbia University Press.
Cienki, Alan. 2018. "Insights for Linguistics and Gesture Studies from Film Studies. A View from Researching Cinematic Metaphor." In *Cinematic Metaphor in Perspective. Reflections on Cinematic Metaphor*, edited by Sarah Greifenstein, Dorothea Horst, Thomas Scherer, Christina Schmitt, Hermann Kappelhoff, and Cornelia Müller, 53–68. Berlin/Boston, MA: Walter de Gruyter.
Cienki, Alan, and Cornelia Müller, eds. 2008. *Metaphor and Gesture*. Amsterdam: John Benjamins.
Coëgnarts, Maarten, and Peter Kravanja. 2012. "Embodied Visual Meaning. Image Schemas in Film." *Projections. The Journal for Movies and Mind* 6 (2): 84–101.
Coëgnarts, Maarten, and Peter Kravanja. 2014. "Metaphor, Bodily Meaning, and Cinema." *Special issue of Image [&] Narrative* 15 (1): 1–4.
Fahlenbrach, Kathrin. 2007. "Embodied Spaces. Film Spaces as Leading Audiovisual Metaphors." In *Narration and Spectatorship in Moving Images*, edited by Joseph D. Anderson and Barbara Fisher Anderson, 105–124. Cambridge: Cambridge Scholar Press.
Fahlenbrach, Kathrin. 2008. "Emotions in Sound. Audiovisual Metaphors in the Sound Design of Narrative Films." *Projections. The Journal for Movies and Mind* 2 (2): 85–103.
Fahlenbrach, Kathrin. 2010. *Audiovisuelle Metaphern. Zur Körper- und Affektästhetik in Film und Fernsehen*. Marburg: Schüren.
Fahlenbrach, Kathrin. 2016a. "Audiovisual Metaphors as Embodied Narratives in Moving Images." In *Embodied Metaphors in Film, Television, and Video Games. Cognitive Approaches*, edited by Kathrin Fahlenbrach, 33–50. New York, NY: Routledge.
Fahlenbrach, Kathrin. 2016b. *Embodied Metaphors in Film, Television and Video Games. Cognitive Approaches*. New York, NY: Routledge, Taylor & Francis Group.
Fahlenbrach, Kathrin. 2017a. "Audiovisual Metaphors and Metonymies of Emotions and Depression in Moving Images." In *Metaphor in Communication, Science and Education*, edited by Francesca Ervas, Elisabetta Gola, and Maria Grazia Rossi, 95–118. Berlin/Boston, MA: De Gruyter.
Fahlenbrach, Kathrin. 2017b. "Sonic Spaces in Movies. Audiovisual Metaphors and Embodied Meanings in Sound Design." In *Body, Sound and Space. Multimodal Exploration*, edited by Clemens Wöllner, 129–149. New York, NY: Routledge.
Forceville, Charles. 2011. "The JOURNEY Metaphor and the Source-Path-Goal Schema in Agnès Varda's Autobiographical GLEANING Documentaries." In *Beyond Cognitive Metaphor Theory. Perspectives on Literary Metaphor*, edited by Monika Fludernik, 281–297. London: Routledge.
Forceville, Charles. 2017. "From Image Schema to Metaphor in Discourse. The FORCE Schemas in Animation Films." In *Metaphor. Embodied Cognition and Discourse*, edited by Beate Hampe, 239–256. Cambridge: Cambridge University Press.
Forceville, Charles, and Marloes Jeulink. 2011. "The Flesh and Blood of Embodied Understanding. The Source-Path-Goal Schema in Animation Film." *Pragmatics & Cognition* 19 (1): 37–59.
Gibbs, Raymond W., Jr. 2006. *Embodiment and Cognitive Science*. New York, NY: Cambridge University Press.

Goldstein, Bruce. 2010. *Sensation and Perception*. Belmont: Wadsworth.
Grodal, Torben K. 1997. *Moving Pictures. A New Theory of Film Genres, Feelings and Cognition*. Oxford: Clarendon Press.
Grodal, Torben K. 2009. *Embodied Visions. Evolution, Emotion, Culture, and Film*. New York: Oxford University Press.
Johnson, Mark. 1987. *The Body in the Mind. The Bodily Basis of Meaning, Imagination, and Reason*. Chicago, IL: University of Chicago Press.
Kappelhoff, Hermann, and Sarah Greifenstein. 2016. "Audiovisual Metaphors. Embodied Meaning and Process of Fictionalization." In *Embodied Metaphors in Film, Television, and Video Games*, edited by Kathrin Fahlenbrach, 183–201. New York, NY: Routledge.
Kappelhoff, Hermann, and Cornelia Müller. 2011. "Embodied Meaning Construction. Multimodal Metaphor and Expressive Movement in Speech, Gesture, and Feature Film." *Metaphor and the Social World* 1 (2): 121–153.
Koppe, Simo, Susanne Harder, and Mette Vaever. 2008. "Vitality Affects." *International Forum of Psychoanalysis* 17: 169–179.
Kövecses, Zóltan. 2003. *Metaphor and Emotion. Language, Culture, and Body in Human Feeling*. Cambridge: Cambridge University Press.
Lakoff, George. 1987. *Woman, Fire, and Dangerous Things. What Categories Reveal About the Mind*. Chicago, IL: Chicago University Press.
Marks, Laura. 2000. *The Skin of the Film. Intercultural Cinema, Embodiment, and the Senses*. Durham: Duke University Press.
Müller, Cornelia. 2008. "What Gestures Reveal About the Nature of Metaphor." In *Metaphor and Gesture*, edited by Alan Cienki and Cornelia Müller, 219–245. Amsterdam: John Benjamins.
Müller, Cornelia, and Hermann Kappelhoff. 2018. *Cinematic Metaphor. Experience – Affectivity – Temporality*. In collaboration with Sarah Greifenstein, Dorothea Horst, Thomas Scherer, and Christina Schmitt. Berlin/Boston, MA: Walter de Gruyter.
Nannicelli, Ted, and Paul Taberham. 2014. *Cognitive Media Theory*. New York, NY: Routledge, Taylor & Francis Group.
Plantinga, Carl, and Greg M. Smith, eds. 1999. *Passionate Views. Film, Cognition and Emotion*. Baltimore, MA: Johns Hopkins University Press.
Schmitt, Christina, Sarah Greifenstein, and Hermann Kappelhoff. 2014. "Expressive Movement and Metaphoric Meaning Making in Audio-Visual Media." In *Body – Language – Communication. An International Handbook on Multimodality in Human Interaction*, edited by Cornelia Müller, Alan Cienki, Ellen Fricke, Silva H. Ladewig, David McNeill, and Jana Bressem, 2092–2112. Berlin/Boston, MA: De Gruyter Mouton.
Shaviro, Steven. 1994. *The Cinematic Body*. Minneapolis: University of Minnesota Press.
Sobchack, Vivian. 1992. *The Address of the Eye. A Phenomenology of Film Experience*. Princeton, NJ: Princeton University.
Sobchack, Vivian. 2004. *Carnal Thoughts. Embodiment and Moving Image Culture*. Berkeley, CA: University of California Press.
Stern, Daniel N. 1985. *The Interpersonal World of the Infant. A View from Psychoanalysis and Developmental Psychology*. London: Karnac Books.
Stern, Daniel N. 1999. "Vitality Contours. The Temporal Contour of Feelings as a Basic Unit for Constructing the Infant's Social Experience." In *Early Social Cognition. Understanding Others in the First Months of Life*, edited by Philippe Rochat, 67–80. London: Lawrence Erlbaum.

Turner, Mark. 1996. *The Literary Mind*. New York: Oxford University Press.
Urios-Aparisi, Eduardo. 2010. "The Body of Love in Almodóvar's Cinema. Metaphor and Metonymy of the Body and Body Parts." *Metaphor and Symbol* 25 (3): 181–203.
Vaz, Mark Cotta. 2002. *The Art of Star Wars Episode 2. Angriff der Klonkrieger*. Stuttgart: Dino Entertainment.

Anne Eusterschulte
Actio per distans: Blumenberg's Metaphorology and Hitchcock's REAR WINDOW

Wer doch einmal die Geschichte des Fensters schrieb – dieses wunderlichen Rahmens unseres häuslichen Daseins, vielleicht sein eigentliches Maaß, ein Fenster voll, immer wieder ein vollgeschöpftes Fenster, mehr haben wir nicht von der Welt; und wie bestimmt die Form unseres jeweiligen Fensters die Art unseres Gemüths: das Fenster des Gefangenen, die croiseé eines Palastes, die Schiffsluke, die Mansarde, die Fensterrose der Kathedrale –: sind das nicht ebensoviel Hoffnungen, Aussichten, Erhebungen und Zukünfte unseres Wesens?

(Rilke 1977, 315)

[*If only someone would write the history of the window – of this wonderous frame of our domestic existence, maybe his actual size, a window full, always a window full to the brim, that's all we got of the world; and how does the shape of our respective window determine the nature of our minds: the window of the prisoner, the croiseé of a palace, the ship's hatch, the attic, the rose window of the cathedral –: are these not just as much hopes, prospects, uprisings and futures of our being?*]

(Rilke 1977, 315, translation by A.E.)

Figure 1: Complex window dispositions in Alfred Hitchcock's REAR WINDOW.

Note: I would like to thank Daniel Fisher for the careful translation of this text.

https://doi.org/10.1515/9783110615036-006

Metaphorologies of framed worlds

The following reflections attempt to bring together Hans Blumenberg's metaphor theory with conceptual considerations about the "poiesis of film-viewing" (Müller and Kappelhoff 2018) with reference to Alfred Hitchcock's film REAR WINDOW.[1] For developing this, several principles of Blumenberg's metaphorological research method are recalled first. Thereupon, a closer look at a metaphorical complex and its cinematographic appearance shall be taken: windows and the extract character of framed realities. The cinematic procedures of a metaphorical thematization of window situations interlocks modes of visual experiences and temporality, and brings reflections on threshold situations into focus. These cinematically manifold connoted stagings of a transitory potential will be correlated by way of conclusion with Blumenberg's modelling of the *actio per distans*.

Views of life-worlds – metaphorological framings

In the context of his redefining of the function of rhetoric, Blumenberg conceives the uses of metaphors as manners of the linguistic negotiation of human relationships with the world. Metaphors are subsequently not, for example, a linguistic means which merely serves as speech embellishment and rhetorical decor, characteristics which would suggest metaphor's dispensability. Nor are they to be reduced to a persuasive, affect-stimulating response function, even though the rhetoric of affects will surely enjoy an important role when one approaches film with the research method of metaphorology. And, finally, the function of metaphors will not be dealt with adequately as long as they are qualified as an expression of matters of fact *not yet* conceptually defined, as if they were something like tentative pictorial formula for objects whose precise conceptual determination had yet to be made. Altogether contrary to such attributions, as a significant element of rhetoric the metaphor possesses for Blumenberg both a constitutively anthropological and pragmatic function. That means that it eventuates culturally with its "surplus of expressive achievement" (Blumenberg 2010 [1960], 3) when conceptual definitions find themselves in an awkward situation because the subject, toward which they point, either resists human explanatory power, or strikes it in its uncertainty with fear. This disquietude has to be subdued through language. Following Blumenberg, especially the so-called "absolute metaphors"

---

[1] Cf. also Müller and Kappelhoff 2018 for an analysis of REAR WINDOW and the poiesis of film-viewing.

(Blumenberg 2010 [1960], 3) fulfill this function. They can be described as linguistic ways of dealing with totalities which are not an object of experience and which thus quite literally cannot be grasped, as when, for instance, one talks about a *self* or *life*, or refers to *history* or the *world*. When human thought operates with metaphorical vocabulary, then this has rather deep existential reasons, because it has to do with questions which we find "already *posed* in the ground of our existence" (Blumenberg 2010 [1960], 14), hence questions around irreducible challenges which are not to be silenced.

It is in this sense that processes of appropriation of the world or coming to terms with reality can be observed with metaphors. The rhetorical forms attest to how localizations of humans in the world are formed and regimes of sense are founded in light of the confrontation with a reality which comes across to human beings as foreign, overwhelming, disparate or contingent. Not least as a manner of reaction to metaphysically unsolved questions – about horizons of meaning and significance, with regards to the situatedness of human life within the world as a whole or rather with respect to the experience of the finitude of human life – metaphors become functionally relevant (Blumenberg 2010 [1960], 13). They are initially constituting spheres and possibilities for action.

Whereas Blumenberg concentrates in his programmatic early writings on these metaphysical challenges and on the metaphorical register of answers in the context of processes pertaining to intellectual history and the history of science, in his later writings the phenomena of an everyday speech metaphor becomes ever more apparent. By taking metaphors into account in a way that is oriented towards the "connections [*rückwärtige Verbindungen/rearward connection*] with the life-world as the constant motivating support (though one that cannot be constantly kept in view) of all theory" (Blumenberg 1997 [1979], 81), the virulence of unanswerable questions appears in different perspectivation. Indeed, even if human query has left the expectation of a scientifically or conceptually exact foundation of truth behind and has learned to live with this disappointment, so it remains to at least ask why the questionability itself, the uncertainty allows no peace of mind. This 'Motivierungsrückhalt' [*motivational retention*] undermines the pragmatic executions of life-worldly actions. Still, that we cannot cast off the queries and continue to put semantic expectations to the world, reveals itself as a continually enervating, latently disruptive element which time and again manages a breakthrough. In this sense, metaphors for Blumenberg are, formulated figuratively, "fossils that indicate an archaic stratum of the trial of theoretical curiosity" (Blumenberg 1997 [1979], 82), i.e., fossils of language which refer to a deep layer of human experience with questionability. Through metaphors we experience something about the horizons of life-worldly expectations and 'attitudes', as well as about approaches to lending meaning to the life-world. In this sense, the metaphor recounts something about a life-worldly experience or rather how this is perceived. "It is difficult to think it away, out of the life-worldly attitude that *precedes* and *underlies all theory* in our history, and it should be kept in mind, looking back if only because it invites us to see the mere use value of the world, mediated by the instrument of science as a secondary direction taken by the theoretical attitude" (Blumenberg 1997 [1979], 86, italics A.E.)

The primary sense of direction of metaphors or life-worldly motivational retention from metaphors is in fact expression of an expectation. For Blumenberg it becomes critical to see how in the historical change of such metaphors expectations appear which are pointing to the life-world.

This primary sense of direction, that is to say, historical surroundings and semantic expectations but also disappointments, proceeds through history in metaphors. It continuously connotes the functional expectations of orientation with metaphorical speech and gives each actual use something like an historical backbone of semantic expectations; they reveal something about the unredeemed, disappointed expectations and thereby about attitudes toward the world in cultural anthropological change. Metaphors carry in themselves a biography of questionabilities and coping attempts.

> Therefore, if metaphorology does not want to limit itself to the contribution that metaphor makes to concept formation but takes it instead as the guiding thread for consideration of the life-world, it will not get by without inserting itself into the wider horizon of a theory of nonconceptuality [*Theorie der Unbegrifflichkeit*]. (Blumenberg 1997 [1979], 88)

Thus, with Blumenberg we can note what is the capacity of metaphorical forms which function similar to concepts: they frame and – with rhetorical forms of expression and visual formulae – border the non-conceptual or zones of indeterminacy. And they do this in a way by which an orientation-founding area for action and mutual understandig emerges, where demands for action of life-wordly relevance can be met. Metaphors manifest social realities, normative orders and cultural expectations. They reveal themselves as pragmatic structuring or provisional facilities within a reality which discloses no reliable indications of its true conditions. In this way, models of reality always indicate forms of negotiation and reflection on the reliability of cognitive possibilities (Blumenberg 1979 [1964], 29–48).

Yet insofar as such assurances about shared life-worlds at the same time have to do with historical perspectives, alternative or contrasting world views are always also possible or present as parallel concepts for negotiation. Thus, metaphorical conceptualizations sensitize for the projective possibility of different worlds, they appear in the shape of hybridizations and linguistic transgressions of the "sayable" ("Sprengmetaphoriken"). Above all, they become for Blumenberg rhetorical forms of expression of delay, of extension or of suspension of an immediate, reactive need for action. For this reason, metaphors are in no case to be situated exclusively on the linguistic level, taking shape rather in and from lifeworlds and hence affecting continually lived, interpersonal practices.

Yet a merely tentative dependability characterizes the metaphor. Metaphors constitute temporary test arrangements of shared realities. Metaphors are pragmatic, which is to say they guarantee no timeless truth but rather time-bound ways of consensus building. But that means as well that the metaphorical conceptualizations of action are subordinate to change over time; they provoke 'Umbesetzungen' [*reallocations*] even when the models of negotiation lose credit, when existential challenges in dealing with the question of the temporality of life or the concern about the human self-conception necessitate renewed stabilization.

This also applies for metaphorical complexes, called by Blumenberg "metaphors of existence". Consider, for example, the metaphorical complex of existence as a crossing on the sea of life, shipwreck with spectator, or metaphors of transgression like care that crosses the river (Blumenberg 2010 [1979]).

One such metaphor of existence which thematizes the relation to the temporality of existence or of its transparency, articulates itself as well in the metaphor which we wish to highlight here: viewing windows and window views.

Let us then ask whether and how these attempted answers, culturally and historically coded ever anew, are effective in responding to unresolved questions of human self- and world-conception in the medium of film or in filmic metaphors. That does not only mean sensitizing for manifold cultural connotations which are present in filmic images, but above all becoming attentive to the functional dimension, in other words, reflecting on the questionability of ostensibly self-evident points of view and ways of thinking. In the course of this it also has to do with strategies which evoke the viewer's affective involvement and release a free play of the imagination. The so provoked dynamic of 'aberrations' and 'deviations' of thought – to play on Blumenberg's terminologies – which is set in motion by the cinematic image, points far away from a representational reference to reality, in a plural sense to *Wirklichkeiten, in denen wir leben* [*realities in which we live*] (Blumenberg 1981). Following Blumenberg, these realities are always first constituted, expressions of perspectivations on a reality which can in no sense count as given, empirical facticity.

In this sense, cinematic images show a specific mode of relating oneself to objective experiences and instances. Through the multi-sensory process of perception they create blueprints of reality. They react to the questionability of the given via perspectives which initiate possibilities of understanding but also irritate, equally putting into play and at risk their cultural historical prerequisites. And perhaps it necessitates an occasionally criminological sense and a distant vantage point – which Blumenberg names *actio per distans* – to become aware of this poiesis of realities, its potentialities and eventualities. All this takes time and requires distance taking delay.

Modes of temporality and time perception come likewise into focus in Hitchcock's film REAR WINDOW. It remains to be shown how reflection here on modes of seeing, on modes of the investigation in perspective or of the framing of visible and invisible realities, is pictured audiovisually.

Window situations and rearwardness [*Rückwärtigkeit*]

In REAR WINDOW, the continuous reflection on cinematic and photographic seeing, and the production thereby of images and of associative idea complexes is obvious and ubiquitous. It is a reflection and production that in no way is reducible to a representational function but rather leaves open for discussion manners of understanding and outlooks on reality, challenging spectators affectively and intellectually. In what follows the main point is not to undertake a comprehensive analysis of the film or of the storyline. It is, rather, the intention – and this, too, by way of a mere few observations – to take a close look at the correlation of a multi-layered perspective (as regards visual experience and time perception) with a central figurative element: window situations.

That the cinematic examination of the glance from or into the window as framing of perceptions of reality and their temporalities plays a central role, is already suggested by the title: REAR WINDOW. The rear-fitted or rearward-turned window draws attention not only to a spatial backward directedness, as it opens onto a back courtyard, but also figuratively to a temporal turning back, a retrospective. And here already metaphorical connotations and the interlacing of temporality with modes of visual experience or of imaginative seeing meet with friction. Let us focus on metaphorical shifts in meaning of these framed realities and therewith on window situations in the sense which Blumenberg calls metaphorical complex, and recall the aforementioned elucidation:

> It is difficult to think it away, out of the life-worldly attitude that *precedes* and *underlies all theory* in our history, and it should be kept in mind, looking back if only because it invites us to see the mere use value of the world, mediated by the instrument of science as a secondary direction taken by the theoretical attitude. (Blumenberg 1997 [1979], 86)

The theoretical conduct has also yet another sense of direction, one of primary relevance. Call it an outlook, one bound to the life-worldly, on potentials of the experientially accessible experience. It combines both a retrospective connection to former events and an orientation toward possible future events. Such a sense of possibility plays a crucial role in Hitchcock's film. It manifests itself, for instance, in a detective-like and criminological investigation of cinematic scenes, an examination directed towards a crime. These scenes are staged as evidence of a continuing, extensive long-term observation, in which occurrences fit together piece by piece in anticipation of the future. At the end, we know that Thorwald actually murdered his wife.

However, in the long enduring observation process it is at first conjectures, projections and scenarios of a possible event, which spectators traverse with the protagonist. And it is crucial that backward-looking ideas of what could have occurred and forward-looking considerations of what will ensue determine the cinematic event and spectators' imagination alternately. Notions of possibilities within a framed world, the life-world of a courtyard setting, which as a self-contained cosmos of action with introduced dramatis personae is, at it were, a sphere of plausibility which delimits the spatial and temporal order. Yet at the same time this framework permits diverse conceptual possibilities for contexts of the plot which are equally capable of appearing rationally plausible.

In his reflections concerning the cosmological metaphor of 'possible worlds', i.e., concerning the displacement of the idea of the world as a sole and unified cosmos, Blumenberg made an observation which in a figurative sense can be brought to bear on the 'microcosm' of the courtyard situation. "One can formally observe how the plural of world, dismissed and released from its genuine cosmological function and usability, now develops into an instrument of novel statements, as a metaphor for the plurality of human worlds [*Menschenwelten]*" (Blumenberg 2007), but which at the same time claims a common foundation or order. But these cultural worlds open up particularly on the level of aesthetics of the imaginable – and here the metaphor comes into play: "With its multiplicability, the world has lost everything that can be understood by analogy of a thing or object of experience. [...] But just as it has become an idea of the totality of possible experience, not the concept of an object of experience, it is accessible to metaphorical 'heteronomy' [*metaphorische 'Fremdbestimmung'*]." (Blumenberg 2007, 72, translation by A.E.) The imaginable worlds of experience provoke directly metaphorical models of comprehension. Recourse to Nietzsche might make this thought clear: "Nietzsche first combined the expression metaphor with the expression world by speaking of 'metaphor worlds' [*Metaphernwelten*]. (Werke VI 57) There is a connection here: because word metaphors exist and must exist" – ways, in other words, of being able to apprehend reality as shared life-world – and "because this is a vacancy to the term that can only be fulfilled by the imagination, therefore metaphors unite to form metaphor worlds with their own logic of association, their pictorial covering and touch, which can, however, [...] have a superficial incompatibility." (Blumenberg 2007, 74, translation by A.E.)

It appears to be a benefit of the concept to conceive abstract models of the world. And as a matter of fact, the concept is for Blumenberg evident anthropologically as "Organ of the *perceptio per distans*" (Blumenberg 2007, 75, translation by A.E.) therefore as a faculty of reason to gain distance from the objects of perception, a perception of retaining distance which opens up a horizon which points well beyond the mere sensorial given:

> Such an expanded horizon not only contains what concerns or will affect the perceiving system acutely, but also contains all sorts of things that could affect it. The instruments for the possibility must be much more extensive than those for acute, i.e. bodily and body-like reality. (Blumenberg 2007, 75, translation by A.E.)

Conceptually operating reason carries out a broadening of the horizon, over the distance from the rush of sensory afflictions. The conceptually apprehended world is a product of backing away, of abstraction. It draws up a realm of the possible, makes the world reliable in anticipation of these possibilities and precludes the impossible. It consequently brings relief in a way from imponderable horrors, from the direct sensory-bodily confrontation with reality as from an uncertain hereafter. Moreover, the concept can represent the absent, that which is not at all present in the direct experience, and preventively assign to it a sensible place. Here one could maintain that with this conceptual broadening of the horizon and the rational anticipation of the possibility spectrum, the use of metaphors has become superfluous. But Blumenberg noticed just the opposite. "One should think that the abstract concept, where it reaches its extreme performance, is least in need of the metaphor or lets the surrogate need of visualization be felt the least. But just the opposite is true" (Blumenberg 2007, 77, translation by A.E.) In the highest degree of abstraction, conceptual reason reaches its limitations; accordingly, the resolution of the immediate sensory view qua conceptual rationalization leads back to the view, to the use of metaphors as aesthetic medium. "The metaphor is the instrument of an expansive world relationship" (Blumenberg 2007, 88, translation by A.E.), it creates frames in its surpluses of meaning and its luxuriating gestural language something which leads beyond the achievements of conceptual reason and returns perhaps for just this reason to the challenges of the life-world which find in the abstract concept no or not enough satisfaction.

Blumenberg's phenomenological observation of anthropological modellings of being-in-the-world is aimed at the "peculiar reference of our imagination to what has not yet been understood." (Blumenberg 2007, 107, translation by A.E.) It is not least the imaginative wealth which articulates itself metaphorically and first creates imaginative free spaces. When Blumenberg states that the metaphor links "the language areas of the *primary relationship to reality* and the *secondary relationship of possibility*" (Blumenberg 2007, 88, translation by A.E.), the task then is to follow here the rhetoric of cinematic language to the complex of metaphors of the window.

Views from the window and imagined parallel worlds

Already the initial scenes of the film open a temporally multi-directional and audiovisually multi-sensory experience. In the opening credits of REAR WINDOW we are led to look through a window. Window shades are rolled up successively on three parties of a display window, noticeable from the perspective of a room inside. While the notification text is still rolling over the input image, it becomes increasingly bright. The window facing the yard appears bit by bit behind the opened blinds illuminated by daylight. Moreover, through the last of the blinds opening like a theater curtain, the courtyard situation with its window facades shines through. Daybreak as a threshold situation, but also as a transition between sleeping and waking, is dramatized with the semitransparent interweaving of inner and outer space. The window as experiential realm of the threshold is already indicated as a metaphor of a transitory moment.

A tracking shot moves the view from an opened window into the courtyard, showing the spatial arrangement of an enclosed backyard where only one narrow corridor on the left side opens up to the street, pointing to an outer world beyond the dominant enclosed space. Above the backdrop of multistorey apartment houses is a piece of sky, allowing the different times of day to be experienced.

Apart from that, the camera and thus the gaze remains focused on the courtyard situation, at once an indoor and outdoor space. Like in an exposition, we become acquainted with the *dramatis personae*, the 'scene' of the event and the immediate circumstances outside in the yard by looking through the camera at a distance.

The continuous movement between inside and outside, insights and outlook, which hereafter, through the window motifs, the film as a whole establishes as a poly-semantic metaphor for crossing thresholds, becomes experienceable here in the film's beginning with the return of the camera-lead view to the interior, a room. At the same time, however, what takes place is an experience of examining spatial and temporal thresholds or, rather, threshold perceptions of consciousness.

The protagonist comes into view for the first time in a close-up of a face covered in perspiration, followed by the shifting to a leg in a cast: "Here lie the broken bones of L.B. Jefferies." Fractured time, irruption of uncontrollable events. We still don't know him, the wheelchair-bound protagonist, who is soon after introduced as a photo reporter who is forced by an accident to take seven weeks' leave from his risky life as reporter of crisis situations the world over. Poised in this waiting position he becomes a witness from the window. The ringing of an alarm clock, the sounds of radio in the courtyard, life awakening by daybreak and with it the opening of time windows, all this comes into play in the alternating of indoor and outdoor image sequences. The still anonymous camera eye makes us witnesses of everything going on before promptly taking the perspective of the protagonist. From then on we will see with his eyes.

But before that we fathom the room, coming into contact with modellings of time measurement or with different mediums of temporality. A fever thermometer as a measuring instrument for the protagonist's daily mental state, alarm clock sounds which send a reminder to rise, radio messages to men over forty. The camera leads through the room inside, lets the view fall to a photo camera, wanders the walls where black-and-white photos document the eye witnessing of war and crisis events, like souvenir pictures or shards past which we are led to for brief moments, which nonetheless trigger associations at once. Suggestively the film camera leads past that and leaves it to the viewers to make for themselves out of these indices a picture of situations and of the historical background of the photographer, who is for his part surrounded by his four walls and fixated on the window to the courtyard. Notions about historical instances come together fragmentarily, both by means of the documents in the room inside as well as, alternately, by means of the edged, episodic glimpses of the life outlines from the window scene in the courtyard, presumably fitting together for the viewer little by little. These are backward looking glances which point to a future not yet fulfilled from the perspective of the here and now or of the competence of a protagonist who is virtually condemned to wait and from who, from this on-hold position, is on a look-out: "Six week sitting in a two-room apartment with nothing to do but look out of the windows at the neighbors."

The film camera then identifies itself as medium of the moving image (in color), highlighting its essential difference to a fixed photographic picture (black-white) which really cuts out a historical now, setting it in still-standing images. The cutout character of the respective standpoint-related framings of events reflects modes of witnessing. The photographs attest to realities ephemerally captured on film, as well as being documents for a photographer's testimony: moments of a past experience, time windows. (Figure 2)

Actio per distans: Blumenberg's Metaphorology and Hitchcock's REAR WINDOW —— **103**

Figure 2: Photographs as retrospects in REAR WINDOW.

Likewise, a portrait photo of a female likeness produced with reversed black-and-white negative processing comes into view (Figure 3). The framed photo stands on a table beside fashion journals on whose covers just this face appears positively: allusions to a reversal of perceptual experiences in the image and simultaneously an introduction to the fiancée Lisa.

Little by little we get to know that the protagonist broke his leg in an accident and that future expectations of a possible marriage, a commitment to a possible

Figure 3: Allusions to a reversal of perceptual experiences and an introduction of the protagonist's fiancée Lisa (REAR WINDOW).

life of matrimony, provoke his unmistakable wavering and shying away. There is a delay in action and time, which is justified through the accident. With this distancing from restless life time can be won.

The change of perspectives, between indoor and outdoor spaces, room situation, window view and courtyard sight, between past events and expectations for the future, this threshold between past and the not-yet opens up rooms of possibility for an imaginable future and thus different perspectives on the visible and the potentials inhering in it. That these open possibilities harbor at the same time projective expectations is indicated through the words of the characteristically farsighted nurse Stella: "I got a nose for trouble."

In the course of the film diverse modes of visual experience, sharpness of vision, clarity, close-up and distant views, or the shifting of standpoints through the staging of different viewing frameworks, become thematic time and again. Not only the window as a framed outlook and insight hints at the continual reflection on seeing. The continual change in perspective manifests itself similarly through visual instruments like a pair of binoculars or the photo camera which the protagonist picks up, as well as mirror images. For example, when the seeing instance (the eye, binoculars, camera, slide) and the event appear reflected in each another. (Figure 4)

The spatial perspectives, the closing in (zoom) or digression of the view, sharpness and depth or breadth of vision, point figuratively to dispositions of the active imagination, of recollection or of the realization of the forthcoming. The

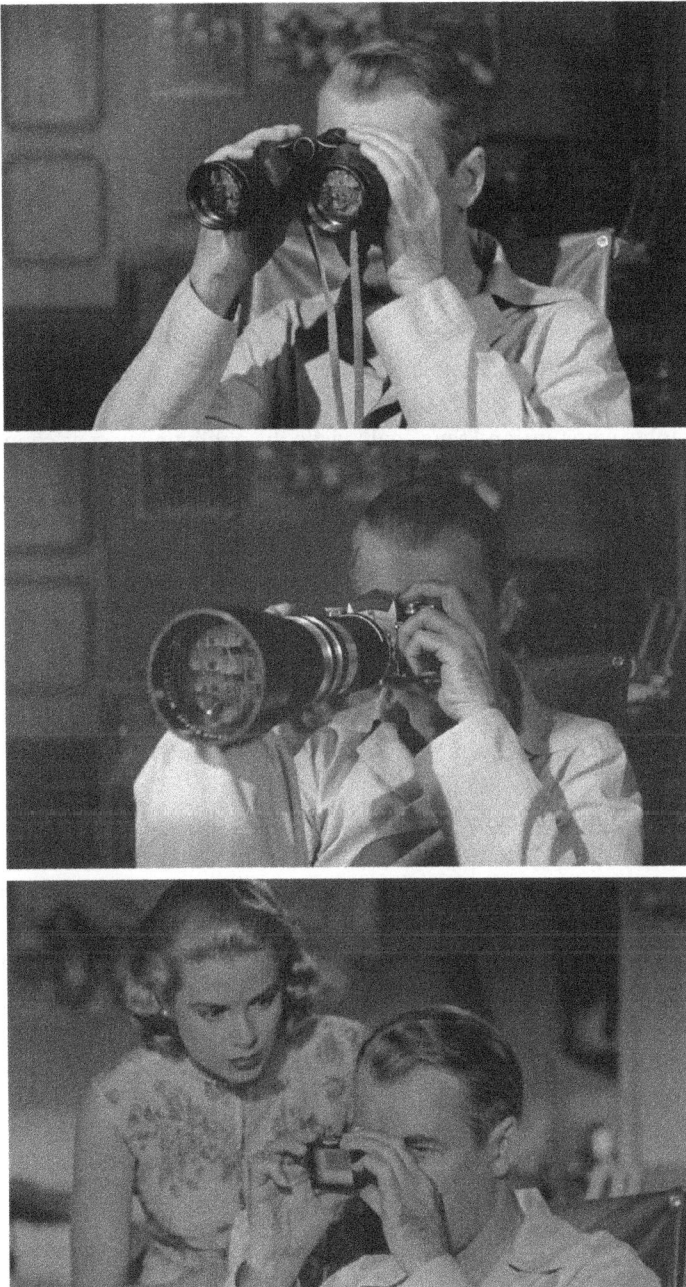

Figure 4: A continual reflection on looking through windows and mirroring windows in REAR WINDOW.

window becomes a metaphor of psychic dispositions and points to past histories like to mutually confronting life realities, a basic theme running through the film. Attention is repeatedly led to the transfer between waking and semiconscious states of the active imagination. Repeatedly the protagonist Jeff is seen falling asleep, only to wake with a start, being on the alert again within a second for the sequenced occurrence. The alternating between daytime and nighttime or light and dark situations underscores this.

These disruptions of viewing experiences are steadily interspersed with figures of delay, of postponement in the face of existential decisions. The immobilized life of a world traveling photo journalist who given his injury is stuck in this room and who for boredom can do nothing other than to make observations from the window, and the way of life of a mundane woman, a desired object of fashion photography, who time and time again visits the oubliette, meet as counterparts. The promise of marriage, forever stalled, not or unforeseeably to be fulfilled, and the challenge of synchronizing two completely divergent ways of life, becomes a figure of one such suspension, that is, of the temporal gain in distance.

Against this backdrop the courtyard scenes appear like commentaries or variations on one theme. On each one of these opened window stages, glimpses into ways of life, into couple relationships in different stages of life are presented. The protagonist's secretly watchful and observant eye maintains something voyeuristic, yet at the same time we are confronted with a pluralization of possible lifeworlds and models which are played out concurrently. Here as well the cutout character of the window frames, the presentation of scenes from a life, virtually invite us to envision imaginatively what is behind the scenes and what is going to happen or follow when the actors exit the window stage once more. Through the ongoing and repeated sights of these window worlds, which, however, always only come into view with temporal interruptions, varieties of life models which can be readily devised imaginatively fill the voids, the shielded between the sequences of these episodic novels. The stage-like opened window presents scenes, but more than anything it conceals.

Meanwhile, we have with these introductory considerations which make the film tangible already drawn closer to the metaphorical complex of the rearview window.

REAR WINDOW – Cinematography of a metaphorical complex

Blumenberg did not concern himself in his metaphorological studies with cinematic images or metaphors relating to the medium of film. That a metaphorological perspective sensitizes us to a surplus of meaning, as with the spaces for imaginative free play and the rhetorics of visualization, may have already been indicated in the considerations about visual thresholds and the thematization of time relationships. The observation at a distance is essential, as evoked in the film continually and through the change in settings. In closing we will return once more to the role of the metaphor in the course of *actio per distans*, action at a distance.

To begin we focus on the metaphorical complex on which aesthetic perception and philosophical time considerations concentrate: the window as framework for visual worlds, i.e., for a reflection on visual experiences and visual perspectives, by which the multi-sensorial experiences are set in scene. In this context, it is particularly the film music which becomes effective as medium of different temporalities and tenses and evokes emotional dispositions.

But let's initially turn to a literary text for making a first approach to overlapping meanings of a complex metaphor; in the process we are led back to Hitchcock's film. In a 1902 letter from Paris, the poet Rilke writes to his wife about hotel rooms he has come upon and relates these to his present hotel accommodation:

> Both were smaller than my current room, which is actually large, only very low, and they had the advantage of allowing this vastness of vision, the width outside the windows; that was, besides the tidiness, the most compelling thing for me, because my hotel, no matter how many drawbacks it may have, its main is this narrow alleyway with the windows vis-á-vis, with all those framed moments of other people's lives, whose witness you are constantly forced to be, especially in the moments when one directs one's gaze into the distance. Tight encounters that frighten. And if you also consider that all these 12 windows I have in front of me, sitting at my desk, are not only frames, but also eyes that are open to my life, then it is sometimes hardly bearable. (Rilke 1930, 50–51, translation by A.E.)

Of interest to us here is the description of a multi-perspective window situation, of being situated at and in the window, as backdrop for Hitchcock's film and a metaphorological interpretation. With Rilke it is the vis-à-vis situation, one of seeing face-to-face, in which the house facades and window fronts are confronted with one another over the distance of a narrow alleyway. In taking literally the talk about facades or fronts, it is apparent then that visual metaphors have already been invoked; they point to the face (Fr. *façade* or Lat. *facies*) or to the 'confrontation' as a facing one another. The window-framed cutouts of different life-worlds obtain with Rilke a quite activating potential, inasmuch as they unavoidably come into view and seem themselves to be looking. In the frame they are pictures; just think of a framed portrait, photographic snapshots or film stills, which take as an excerpt from the life-world a moment and expose the life of others to view. However, in film these images don't stand still, but rather present living images. In looking and uncovering, for its part a temporal seeing, in this inspection a moving image always comes into view, even if on the other side not much moves or happens. It is nonetheless a *moment* – a period within which a movement takes place, which is captured here in window frames.[2]

Seeing as a process is reflected in many ways: seeing sets distancing as a prerequisite, in Blumenberg's sense an *actio per distans*. Only the taking of distance (no matter how small) makes it possible for an object to become visible. It gives a necessary spatio-temporal distance to envisage something. What is too close or rests on the eye becomes unclear or invisible. Something needs to stand at a certain distance before our eyes, where sharpness and detail perception or vagueness and haziness compete. But distancing is also a temporal delay in the sense of room for maneuverability gained, one which does not imply immediate reaction, but a postponement of actions instead.

A seeing that cannot elude the object because, owing to a spatial situation, it is confronted with something, provokes inevitably an eyewitness account. But moreover, characteristic for such a seeing is the transcending of boundaries. It catches impermissible glimpses and enters into a private sphere, another life, and in that way acquires something voyeuristic or, as in Hitchcock's case, searches like a detective and is guided by the expectation of something which is already, if in the imagination but still vaguely, looming nonetheless as a secret crime. Finally, the cutout-character of this seeing should be emphasized in the concrete and figurative sense, which manifests itself in window views. Crucial here is not only that all looking – every shot or camera setting – represents an inspection in perspective and thus a subjective view which the viewer shares with the protagonist. With the vision barrier of the window something is hidden, so that here associations and imaginations of the contextual conditions are set in motion. These insights might be frightening, evoking fears, or render entire settings imaginable. The narrowness, the compactness of the seen triggers emotional reactions. Also the viewer that looks out of a window cannot let his or her gaze wander, but instead keeps a lookout from a framework, a frame of vision. And ultimately it is the reciprocity of the window situation which calls attention to seeing as being seen. For

---

[2] In accordance with the counter-motion, described by Michel de Certeau, of distance viewing and crossing (window pane and rail), i.e. the friction of two regimes of visibility, whereby borders dissolve and imaginative space emerge, for Hitchcock the interplay of standing view/window and tracking shot becomes significant. See Certeau (1984 [1980], 112), "Railway Navigation and Incarceration."

Rilke, the windows opposite have eyes so to speak and are themselves glances which find their way into the window of the one glancing: they encounter the viewer's life-world and expose him or her to sight. The window as 'eye of the soul.' In REAR WINDOW, the ones observed frequently come to the window as well and look back (Figure 5).

Figure 5: The reciprocity of the window situation: Seeing as being seen (REAR WINDOW).

One could imagine a furtive look which does not reveal itself. The window functions as a glance through a 'keyhole'.[3] In Hitchcock's film the protagonist occasionally withdraws in the overshadowed background of his lookout room in order to see without being seen. The look out the window across the street continues past a border and at the same time exposes itself to being seen. With these reciprocal visual processes, we become attentive to a process which not only occurs in the private sphere, but which exposes its own position to visibility. In Hitchcock's REAR WINDOW, being situated at the window and looking out of it over the courtyard submits to an interplay, signaling the distancing of an observer's position, but also the danger of being seen, of irritation and fear.

We should remain another moment with these rather phenomenological approaches to a mutual looking *out* of and *in* the window. For it has here to do with a perceiving which so to speak encroaches closely on the visible viewed up close and which with the look *out of the window in the window* transgresses a doubled framework or threshold. With this threshold we approach the metaphor of the window which in many respects invokes just such threshold realms.

The window is itself both an interior and exterior, a phenomenon of alternation which can admit or exclude (be it the level of noise from the outer world or the music emanating from the room into the courtyard and vice versa). As a metaphor, the window stands in multiple ways for the threshold between interior and exterior space, that is, between psychic inner space and the projection into an external realm. For instance, as a glance into the distance, the way Rilke describes it. This distance from afar is, however, a continually framed vista, an outlook both of the ego which is withdrawn in itself, in a room, and of a view wandering out imaginatively toward the distant horizon, subjective. As a framed looking out over the distances of nature, the glance from a window, which transcends the real-world landscape, as in romanticist painting and literature, becomes thematic in manifold ways: as metaphor of subjectivity or inwardness, of reflection on spaces of possibility, dreams and fantasy images. Hence, the window view is no straightforward framed experience of a given reality. It transcends this in the imagination in various ways, allowing imaginative worlds but also deep structures of the visible to be experienced. And this also holds when, in the twentieth century, instead of the natural landscape urban settings come into view from the window, or a far-reaching vista is replaced by a limited close-up of facing house walls or panoramic views which prevent unhindered, unlimited visibility of an open outside.

---

3 Keep in mind the dynamics of the objectifying gaze of the other and becoming seen (shame) in Sartre's phenomenology of the keyhole (Sartre 1956, 252–302).

So, too, does this occur in Hitchcock's REAR WINDOW. The courtyard separating the window fronts from one another is at once interior and exterior space. Window insights and outlooks block the view which roams the expanse, narrows it down to a 'Schauplatz' [*showplace*].[4] And yet the setting of room and courtyard can be seen beyond the representational character of the observed life realities, also as an epitome of an urban sociality, of a packed, ordered life of civilization and its parceling. Living in a box. Modules of life. The viewable calls up fantasies of the invisible. Here different perceptions of space do not only encounter one another but do so continually and simultaneously as temporal dimensions.

The entire courtyard complex obtains with Hitchcock something of a panopticon,[5] of an enclosed social microcosm of observation and control as a structural signature of the modern era. The voyeuristic obtrusiveness also obtains a connotation of morally reprehensible sensationalism, indiscretion and not least of all inaction/inactivity: "New York State's sentence for a Peeping Tom is six months in the work house [...] They've got no windows in the work house. [...] You know in the old days they used to put your eyes out with a red-hot poker. [...] We've become a race of Peeping Toms." So says the ever stable, savvy nurse and seer Stella. (Figure 6)

Figure 6: The courtyard as enclosed social microcosm and theater arena in REAR WINDOW.

---

4 For the history respectively time that enter scene at the 'Schauplatz', see Benjamin (1990 [1928]).
5 For panopticism and prison, see Foucault (1977 [1975], 195–230).

The courtyard also possesses the character of a theater arena, that is, of a combination of many small proscenium stages in a forum which stages parallel stories. In the window views similarly framed life realities run alongside one another, in different time modes and tenses, each with prehistories blended in: time windows.

In many respects, the window is a metaphor of a temporal threshold, an area of transition between times, as between, for example, life and death. In popular belief, for instance in German mythology, there exists the conception that the soul of one deceased departs through the window, having where released from the mortal body to disappear in a super-temporal sphere, on account of which so-called windows of the soul were installed in house facades. As psychologically connoted metaphor, the window stands for ideas of an inspection of spiritual life, the exploration of a person. And this not only because the eyes are, as already seen in the Bible, held as windows of the soul (Math 6,22–23), grounding the belief that the eyes betray inner life. Likewise, with Hitchcock windows can be connoted in the sense of such *eyes* of frameworks of mind. But above all with this opening of inner life there looms a fear of betrayal and self-exposure.

Fantasies of inner life being disclosed through an opening or a window in the breast trace back to Greek mythology and return – in ever new roles – until the modern era. Lucian, for example, reports in *Hermotimus* of a contest between the Greek gods of Minerva, Neptune and Vulcan, for the rank of the most splendid creative capacity for artistic works, which Momus had to determine. Momus, the critic prone to vilify, has something to criticize about every performance; he subjects the god and protector of the blacksmiths Vulcan, who presented as his artwork the human being, to the following reproach: "he should have made a window in his chest, so that, when it was opened, his thoughts and designs, his truth or falsehood, might have been apparent." But with Lucian the thematizing of this antique paragon leads to an astounding consequence. The title-bearing figure of the writing *Hermotimus* is addressed as the epitome of a perfectly poignant gift of profound insight: "but you have sharper eyes than Lynceus, and pierce through the chest to what is inside; all is patent to you, not merely any man's wishes and sentiments, but the comparative merits of any pair" (Lucian of Samosata 1905, pars 21).

This metaphor of inner life transparency is frequently revisited in literature, as the wishful thinking but also horror scenario of a psychological exposure. Naked inner life is open. This connotation as well is one of relevance for Hitchcock's filmic window situations in which human beings disclose their innermost matters and expose themselves. We recall, for instance, the lonely, longing lover (Miss Lonelyhearts) who stages a festive candle-light dinner for an imagined loved one. Longing and loneliness are laid bare through the tangible, cinematically set window.

Actio per distans: Blumenberg's Metaphorology and Hitchcock's REAR WINDOW — **113**

Figure 7: Framed little dramas of everyday-life for the observer in REAR WINDOW.

Figure 7 (continued)

In his reflections on digression as a device of literary writing, Laurence Sterne upholds the assertion that the representation of a character only ever first gains liveliness when the reader learns something in roundabout ways. Everything else would be like things frozen in the winter and would lack any animating force of attraction.

> If the fixure of Momus's glass, in the human breast, according to the proposed emendation of that arch-critick, had taken place, – first, This foolish consequence would certainly have followed, – That the very wisest and the very gravest of us all, in one coin or other, must have paid window-money every day of our lives. And, secondly, That had the said glass been there set up, nothing more would have been wanting, in order to have taken a man's character, but to have taken a chair and gone softly, as you would to a dioptrical bee-hive, and look'd in, – view'd the soul stark naked; – observ'd all her motions, – her

machinations; – traced all her maggots from their first engendering to their crawling forth; – watched her loose in her frisks, her gambols, her capricios; and after some notice of her more solemn deportment, consequent upon such frisks; & – then taken your pen and ink and set down nothing but what you had seen and could have sworn to. (Sterne 2005 [1760], XIII, 65)

In Hitchcock's courtyard we are confronted with one such direct glimpse into the emotional depths of the spiritual landscapes, but also of their imaginative depiction. The windows of the soul show moods, little dramas of the everyday, pair situations or love scenes and life stories: the lonely heart, the gymnastics-prone bathing beauty, the young composer in the attic window ... (Figure 7)

Decisive, however, is that it requires distance and thereby 'digressions' and 'detours' to stage characters. And this is true especially for the affective characterization of the observer, on whose reactions what is seen and expected is emotionally reflected and refractured.

Distance viewing as reflectiveness [*Nachdenklichkeit*]

Winning time is the condition for the possibility of not having to react immediately to confrontations with challenges posed by the oncoming reality. Taking distance opens up room for maneuvering which makes different manners of conduct and courses of action possible, by opening up various ways and above all detours. This is a basic figure of Blumenberg's anthropologically-based formula: *actio per distans*.

Surely, in Hitchcock's cinematic production of the criminological study of distance, the protagonist and his close attachment figures are increasingly drawn into the vortex of a crime ever so slowly revealed. And so are we, the spectators: as witnesses. Yet the film as a process of such focusing is at the same time determined by dynamics of deceleration, tension and postponement. A process of reflection which splits up the promise of marriage, distinct life plans, imagined scenarios of a possible event in the past and future, and, above all, emotional dispositions. The window of the film or film screening is consequently itself a process of the perspective refractions, a play in maintaining distances, and refers accordingly to a cinematic reflectiveness. Delay and postponement are on the one hand a form of emotional and intellectual hesitation – mindful, for instance, of the marriage option – or temporally connoted hesitation, and yet a figure of reflection as of the pleasure or of the intensification qua reflectiveness.

When Blumenberg formulates that "In reflectiveness there is an experience of freedom, especially of freedom of digression. The bandwidth in which to react to digression ranges from the heights of humor to the point of sheer despair of those who want to make progress with a thing" (Blumenberg 1980, 58, translated by A.E.), then this can be understood as a commentary on the film's events. The delay of action, the postponement, the taking of a breath and pausing, without instantly reacting to the challenges of the empirical world, rather first taking a look around, gaining distance in order to reflect, only this creates leeway. Relating to something one way or another also releases an elementary skepticism. For with closer consideration, that means from the distance and with time gain, matters self-evident suddenly reveal themselves as questionable.

And here we should constantly keep an eye on Hitchcock's film and the act of observation, of being on the lookout: criminological fantasy.

Maintaining distance from immediacy provokes delay of action. However, taking one's time to first wait and see carries the risk that things stagnate, that nothing at all happens in the first place – save that further taking-into-account, in a sensorial-perceptual and cognitive sense, yields aberrant, in any event highly unanticipated ideas. Tarrying in rumination liberates something, that means, makes experienceable a freedom which allows one to become aware that there is no necessity to start running after a putative goal, but rather quite possibly to go altogether different routes: *detours*.

> All live strives to give the answers to the questions that arise to him without undue delay and without any harm. [...] Only man affords himself an opposite tendency. He is the being that hesitates. That would be a failure, as life does not forgive it, if the disadvantage would not be compensated by a large expenditure at achievements, the results of which we call experience. That we do not perceive signals but things is based on the fact that we have learned to wait and see, which still shows itself in each case. (Blumenberg 1980, 57, translation by A.E.)

And here as well we might recall a scene from the film. In the face of the protagonist's constant demurring and indecision towards finding his way into a promise of marriage, the nurse's words stand out: "Look, Mr. Jefferies. I'm not an educated woman, but I can tell you one thing – when a man and a woman see each other, and like each other – they oughta come together – wham, like a couple of taxis on Broadway. Not sit around analyzing each other like two specimens in a bottle." Jeff's reply: "There's an intelligent way to approach marriage." But Stella counters: "Intelligence! Nothing has caused the human race so much trouble as intelligence."

As commented in Blumenberg's own words: "Our idea of thinking is that it creates the shortest connection between two points, between a problem and its solution, between a need and its satisfaction, between interests and their consensus –along the discursive line" (Blumenberg 1980, 58, translated by A.E.). But this idea is deceptive because human intelligence is characterized by hesitation.

> Man's deficiency in specific dispositions for reactive behavior vis-à-vis reality – that is, his poverty of instincts – is the starting point for the central anthropological question as to how this creature is able to exist in spite of his lack of fixed biological dispositions. The answer can be reduced to the formula: by not dealing with this reality directly. The human relation to reality is indirect, circumstantial, delayed, selective, and above all *metaphorical* (Blumenberg 1987 [1981], 439)

And in this sense the *cinematic language*, or the poiesis of film-viewing, can be understood as rhetorical, for

> Rhetoric, on the other hand, is, in regard to the temporal texture of actions, a consummate embodiment of retardation. Circumstantiality, procedural inventiveness, ritualization implies a doubt as to whether the shortest way of connecting two points is also the humane route from one to the other. In aesthetics, for example in Music, we are quite familiar with this type of situation. [...we may think of the musical capriccio, of improvisations, strophes and counterparts]. There is a need for an institutionalized catching of breath, which sends even majorities that are competent of make decisions on long rhetorical detours. (Blumenberg 1987 [1981], 445)

Cinematic language and its dialog with spectators would hence be a kind of form of negotiation which intervenes in existing realities, examines microscopically, extrapolates, extracts the life-worldly poetically, but also exposes examination procedures, questioning, where the evidence is lacking.

The metaphor is a figuration of an aesthetic-imaginative detour in the negotiation of life-worlds. And such shifts of views and temporalities, an undermining of finalistic progressions of time, an art of interruption and dynamization is undertaken by the film, for uncovering through imaginative displacements rooms for maneuvering. *One* means of expression for the aesthetic forming of possible worlds of action is the metaphor – here the rear view in window frames:

> "To see you is to love you." (Bing Crosby)

Figure 8: Cinematic reflectiveness and looking through the REAR WINDOW.

Audiovisual sources

REAR WINDOW, Dir. Alfred Hitchcock, Paramount Pictures, USA 1954.

Bibliography

Benjamin, Walter. 1990. *Origin of German Tragic Drama*. Translated by John Osbourne. London: Verso. Original edition 1928.
Blumenberg, Hans. 1979. "The Concept of Reality and the Possibility of the Novel." In *New Perspectives in German Literary Criticism. A Collection of Essays*, edited by Richard E. Amacher and Victor Lange, 29–48. Princeton: Princeton University Press. Original edition 1964.
Blumenberg, Hans. 1980. "Nachdenklichkeit." In *Deutsche Akademie für Sprache und Dichtung. Jahrbuch*, 57–61. Heidelberg.
Blumenberg, Hans. 1981. *Wirklichkeiten, in denen wir leben. Aufsätze und eine Rede*. Stuttgart: Reclam.
Blumenberg, Hans. 1987. "An Anthropological Approach to the Contemporary Significance of Rhetoric." In *After Philosophy. End or Transformation?*, edited by Kenneth Baynes, James Bohman, and Thomas McCarthy, 429–458. Cambridge, MA: MIT Press. Original edition 1981.
Blumenberg, Hans. 1997. "Prospect of a Theory of Nonconceptuality." In *Shipwreck With Spectator. Paradigm of a Metaphor for Existence*, 81–102. Cambridge, MA: MIT Press. Original edition 1979.

Blumenberg, Hans. 2007. *Theorie der Unbegrifflichkeit*. Frankfurt/M.: Suhrkamp.
Blumenberg, Hans. 2010. *Care Crosses the River*. Translated by Paul Flemming. Stanford: Stanford University Press. Original edition 1979.
Blumenberg, Hans. 2010. *Paradigms for a Metaphorology*. Translated by Robert Savage. Ithaca, NY: Cornell University Press and Cornell University Library. Original edition 1960.
Certeau, Michel de. 1984. *Practice of Everyday Life*. Berkeley, CA: University of California Press. Original edition 1980.
Foucault, Michel. 1977. *Discipline and Punish. The Birth of the Prison*. New York: Pantheon Books. Original edition 1975.
Müller, Cornelia, and Hermann Kappelhoff. 2018. *Cinematic Metaphor. Experience – Affectivity – Temporality*. In collaboration with Sarah Greifenstein, Dorothea Horst, Thomas Scherer, and Christina Schmitt. Berlin/Boston: Walter de Gruyter.
Rilke, Rainer Maria. 1930. *Briefe aus den Jahren 1902 bis 1906*. Leipzig: Insel.
Rilke, Rainer Maria. 1977. *Briefe an Nanny Wunderly-Volkart* Vol. 2. Frankfurt/M.: Insel.
Samosata, Lucian of. 1905. "Hermotimus, or the Rival Philosophies." In *The Works of Lucian of Samosata*. Oxford: The Clarendon Press.
Sartre, Jean Paul. 1956. *Being and Nothingness*. Oxford: Philosophical Library.
Sterne, Laurence. 2005. *The Life and Opinions of Tristram Shandy, Gentleman*. Munich: Günter Jürgensmeier. Original edition 1760.

Raymond W. Gibbs, Jr.
Our Metaphorical Experiences of Film

Introduction

Imagine that you are watching an old film, in this case SPELLBOUND (1945, USA) directed by Alfred Hitchcock, which you have never seen before. You are in a darkened theater, totally immersed in what you are observing, including the dialog and soundtrack (as well as some text inserts shown at the beginning of the film). SPELLBOUND is a film noir, psychological thriller that tells the story of a private psychiatric clinic in Vermont, United States, which will now be run by a new director, Dr. Anthony Edwardes, played by Gregory Peck. He seems professionally accomplished, but we soon discover that he suffers from emotional difficulties involving a specific phobia of parallel lines against a solid background. In addition, the man, whose real name is actually John Ballantyne, seems to be an imposter and is believed at one point of being involved with the disappearance, and possible murder, of the real Dr. Edwardes.

John Ballantyne's psychological complexities, which appear at certain places in the film, are apparent to his colleague, and possible love interest, Dr. Constance Petersen, played by Ingrid Bergman. The film has many twists and turns, including a surrealistic dream sequence initially crafted by Salvador Dalí, before coming to a climatic conclusion that reveals the underlying cause of Ballantyne's phobia is related to a traumatic childhood event. Hitchcock sets up this possibility at the very opening of the film when he presents the following description of what was at that point in the United States the new science of psychoanalysis:

> Our story deals with psychoanalysis, the method by which modern science treats the emotional problems of the sane. The analyst seeks only to induce the patient to talk about his hidden problems, to open the locked doors of the mind. Once the complexes that have been disturbing the patient are uncovered and interpreted, the confusion and illness disappear ... And the devils of unreason are driven from the human soul.

In later interviews, most notably with director François Truffaut, Hitchcock stated that his goal was to "turn out the first picture on psychoanalysis", but he expressed disappointment with SPELLBOUND, noting that it was "just another manhunt story wrapped in pseudo-psychoanalysis", and that the film was "too complicated" with a "very confusing ending" (Truffaut 1983, 163, 165–166). Nonetheless, many critics at the time of its 1945 release gave SPELLBOUND very positive reviews. For example, one reviewer noted that the story "was a rather obvious and often-told tale [...] but the manner and quality of its telling is extraordinarily fine [...] the firm texture of the narration, the flow of continuity and dialogue, the shock of the unexpected, the scope of image – all are happily here" (Crowther 1945). Another critic stated, "Very good! [...] The performances of the entire cast are superior, and throughout, the action an overtone of suspense and terror, tinged with touches of deep human interest and appealing romance, is sustained" (N.N. 1945).

Whatever its artistic merits, SPELLBOUND is a metaphorically rich film in multimodal ways (e.g., one sequence shows a series of seven doors opening along a very long hallway after Edwardes/Ballantyne and Petersen first kiss with violins playing in the background).[1] Many films convey metaphorical meanings through multimodal images (e.g., the words spoken, static and moving images presented, soundtrack heard). Many of these multimodal metaphorical messages have a significant role in our in-the-moment sensory experience of a film, as well as our emotional reactions to all that we are seeing and hearing, including possible judgments about a film's plot or narrative. Our memories of a film, such as what we recall about its plot, specific characters and events, and our subjective judgments of a film, are also critically shaped by our experiences of metaphor.

This chapter offers an account of how people construct metaphorical impressions and meanings when watching and later thinking about SPELLBOUND. Metaphor is traditionally viewed as a 'figure of speech' in which a person describes one thing in terms of objects or events from a conceptually dissimilar domain. Alfred Hitchcock offered a telling verbal metaphor regarding the less significant roles that actors had in his films, where the 'script' was everything, when he said "Actors are cattle" (i.e., there to be prodded into doing exactly what Hitchcock's precise script demanded). Still, a revolution in metaphor studies has revealed that metaphor is not only ubiquitous in language, but is also widely present in many nonlinguistic domains, including gesture, music, art, film, dance, and even mathematics (Gibbs 1994, 2017). Indeed, metaphor is vastly multimodal in the sense that a specific metaphorical idea can be exhibited across several modalities (e.g., speech and gesture, speech and music, images and words, images and sounds, words and physical, expressive movement, such as dance) (Forceville and Urios-Aparisi 2009, Cienki and Müller 2008).

My specific claim is that our metaphorical experiences of film dynamically unfold over time from "embodied simulation" processes by which people imaginatively project themselves into the events and human actions they are experiencing in multimodal ways. People create embodied simulations of what other people are saying and doing that involve moment-by-moment "what must it be

---

[1] When Truffaut asked about this scene, Hitchcock replied, "That was terrible!" (Truffaut 1983, 165).

like for other people" processes which make use of ongoing tactile-kinesthetic experiences (Gibbs 2006). These simulations accrue over time as we watch any film that leads to the creation of complex conceptual and affective metaphorical meanings that are deeply grounded in sensory, bodily experiences.

Cinematic expressive movements and embodied simulations

I will explore the emergence of metaphorical experience in film in terms of what Kappelhoff and Müller (2011) describe as "metaphorically orchestrated cinematic expressive movements".

> [C]inematic expressive movements shape the same kind of felt experience in a spectator as a bodily expressive movement that accompanies speech. In doing so, expressive movements provide the experiential grounds for the emergence and construction of metaphors. (Kappelhoff and Müller 2011, 122)

Hermann Kappelhoff, Cornelia Müller, and colleagues have explored the dynamic orchestration of audiovisual compositions in different media, such as TV news reports, advertisements, and film (e.g., see Schmitt, Greifenstein, and Kappelhoff 2014, Müller and Schmitt 2015, Müller and Kappelhoff 2018). For example, one study analyzed the temporal unfolding of metaphor in a six-minute TV news report on the financial crisis in Germany back in 2008 (Müller and Schmitt 2015). A central metaphorical theme that underlies, and orchestrates, the news report is that *winning and losing are experienced and understood as oppositions of many kinds*. Early on in the report, there is a sequence of a group of business consultants at a reception. As the voice-over comments that "business runs brilliantly", the camera focuses on the consultants, standing close together in a circle, lifting their sparkling glasses of champagne high into the air in celebration of their successes. The image of the sparkling glasses lifted high nicely matches the verbal metaphor of "brilliantly" in the voice-over comment, which evokes a specific sensory-motor experience of success as sparklingly light moving upward.

A follow-up sequence presents an interview with one businessman who comments on those bankers who have not succeeded. He comments "These people, who, in fact, high, from high have fallen", and then "… actually, they want to dive away and not be seen," while he is making a downward gesture. These words and gesture create the strong metaphorical impression of losers being down and away from those who have succeeded during the financial crisis. Later on, a group of upset small investors are shown marching down a narrow path, approaching a door on the ground floor of a tall building, ringing the bell, and then talking to someone over an intercom, yet not being allowed into the building. At the end of the sequence, the camera pans upward to higher floors and windows, implying that the successful "winners" are upward and inside, compared to the "losers" who are down and outside.

Most generally, this research program demonstrates how "audio-visual metaphors are dynamic forms of meaning making and are affectively grounded in the sensory experiences of the cinematic expressive movements" (Müller and Schmitt 2015, 336). "What spectators affectively go through when watching a film is intrinsically bound to the way these units, i.e., these movement patterns, unfold dynamically. Different articulatory modalities (e.g., camera movement, montage, or sound) create figurations of movement that establish different gestalt-like forms" (Schmitt, Greifenstein, and Kappelhoff 2014, 2098).

This perspective on metaphor, quite broadly, resists more traditional views that assume metaphor performance and understanding in both linguistic and nonlinguistic domains is primarily accomplished through the recruitment of static metaphorical themes or conceptual metaphors that are stored in individuals' long-term memories (see Gibbs 2017). Instead, looking at metaphorical experiences in film and elsewhere as "metaphorically orchestrated cinematic expressive movements", highlights the dynamic relationship between audiovisual movements in film and people's real and imaginative embodied actions.

My contribution aims to situate the idea of "metaphorically orchestrated cinematic expressive movements" in terms of embodied simulation processes. Our film experiences rely on many similar perceptual and cognitive processes by which we construe meaningful interpretations in the real world. MacDougall (2006, 3) suggested in this regard that the images we construct in film medium are "in a sense mirror of our bodies, replicating the whole of the body's activity, with its physical movements, or shifting attention, and its conflicting impulses toward order and disorder." Much experimental research from perceptual psychology, cognitive psychology, and cognitive neuroscience demonstrates "a continuity between perceiving scenes in movies and in the world, as the dynamics of attention, spatial cognition and action are very similar in direct experience and mediated experience" (Gallese and Guerra 2012, 183, and see research described within Shimamura and Palmer 2012).

Embodied simulations emerge from complex interactions between brains, bodies, and the world in which we use our bodily experiences, past and present, to imaginatively interpret real-world, and perhaps film, events. Consider the following scenario:

> When the plane reached 20,000 feet, John stood up with the other students, tightened the straps of his parachute, and, when it was his turn, he jumped out of the side door.

Our understanding of this scene is accomplished not by simply assembling a list of abstract meaning propositions, but requires us to imagine engaging in the jumping out of the plane action. We experience the sensation of what it may be like to jump out of a plane, even if we have not done this before in real-life. This sensory interpretation does not arise after a purely linguistic analysis of the language has been completed because embodied simulations are an automatic part of the understanding process. Psycholinguistic research supports this account. For example, studies show that people imagine themselves pulling an object toward their bodies when reading "John opened the drawer" and pushing an object away from our bodies when reading "John closed the drawer" (Glenberg and Kaschak 2002).

Part of the neural basis for embodied simulations is seen in the research on 'mirror neurons.' Studies with both humans and non-human primates have shown that motors areas of the brain are activated when individuals see other actors performing different bodily motions (Grafton 2011). These findings imply that people tacitly imagine themselves performing the actions they perceive, which enables them to understand through simulations what other individuals are doing. Simply hearing action-related language, such as the "kick" in "kick the bucket", also activates relevant sensorimotor areas of the brain (i.e., the somatosensory cortex area related to leg actions), once again as if listeners were partially performing the action implied by the verb (Pulvermüller 2013).

One of the initial criticisms of embodied simulation theory is that it could not account for how people think abstractly or use figurative language. But many psycholinguistic studies have shown that embodied simulations play a critical role in our comprehension of abstract and figurative language, such as metaphors and idioms (Bergen 2012, Gibbs 2006). We understand language as if we imagine ourselves engaging in actions relevant to the words spoken or read, even if these actions are not possible to perform in the real-world. For instance, in one series of studies on metaphorical talk about time, students waiting in line at a café were given the ambiguous statement "Next Wednesday's meeting has been moved forward two days" and then asked "What day is the meeting that has been rescheduled?" (Boroditsky and Ramscar 2002). Students who were farther along in the line (i.e., who had thus very recently experienced more forward spatial motion) were more likely to say that the meeting had been moved to Friday, rather than to Monday. This finding suggests that people's embodied experiences shape their interpretations of the ambiguous metaphorical statement.

Other studies show that people's speeded comprehension of metaphorical phrases like "grasp the concept" were facilitated when they first made, or imagined making in this case, a grasping movement (Wilson and Gibbs 2007). Moving, or imagine moving, a relevant bodily action enhances people's construction of the embodied simulation needed to understand "grasp the concept" and other metaphorical phrases. Another test of the embodied simulation hypothesis asked people to read sentences conveying literal (e.g., "She climbed up the hill"), metaphorical (e.g., "She climbed up in the company"), and abstract (e.g., "She succeeded in the company") meanings (Santana and de Vega 2011). As they read the sentences, participants made single hand movements, up or down, which matched or mismatched the sentence meanings. Analysis of the hand movement times showed that people performed them faster when they matched the meanings for all three types of sentences. This result suggests that both metaphorical and abstract sentence meanings recruit embodied representations related to, in this case, vertical spatial movements.

Neuroscience studies also support the idea that relevant sensorimotor areas of the brain are recruited during verbal metaphor understanding. Reading an abstract transfer statement (e.g., "give the news") activates the motor system exactly as does seeing concrete transfer expressions (e.g., "give the pizza") (Glenberg et al. 2008). When people read metaphorical action phrases, such as "grasp the concept", there was nearly identical activation in motor areas of the brain as when participants saw literal action statements (e.g., "John grasped the straw") (Desai et al. 2011). Listening to taste metaphors (e.g., "She looked at him sweetly") or auditory metaphors (e.g., "Her limousine was a privileged snort") also showed an increased activation in relevant somatosensory brain areas (Citron and Goldberg 2014). This body of empirical findings is consistent with the claim that people interpret abstract and metaphorical language in terms of imaginative reenactments of the events referred to in the speech they encounter.

The psycholinguistic and neuroscience literatures clearly show how bodily-based sensory processes are involved in people's understanding of metaphor. Corresponding research also indicates that people's understanding of metaphorical gestures also makes use of sensory processes in relevant areas of the brain (Schippers et al. 2010). Studies also show that listeners readily combine the information from metaphorical words and gestures, with mismatches between the two causing difficulties in both understanding and believing what speakers are communicating (Beattie and Sale 2012).

This scientific work provides the background for my claim that metaphorically orchestrated movements in film may be fundamentally related to embodied simulation processes. I now apply the theory of embodied simulation to describe how people experience film via sensory, embodied processes in eight different segments of SPELLBOUND. This analysis builds off of an earlier discussion of many temporarily-linked metaphorically orchestrated movements in SPELLBOUND (Müller and Kappelhoff 2018, Chapter 13). My primary aim here is to demonstrate that different metaphorically orchestrated movements are dynamically coupled via more localized embodied simulations as they successively accrue during the course of watching SPELLBOUND.

Eight cinematic expressive movements in SPELLBOUND

Early in the film, a female patient is being escorted by an attendant to go meet with her psychiatrist, Dr. Petersen (see Figure 1 top). The woman is chatting, even flirting, with the attendant. When the two of them get to her doctor's office door, the camera moves downward and focuses on her fingernails as she scratches a set of marks across the back of the attendant's hand (see Figure 1 middle). This few seconds of visual action is also accompanied by a soundtrack that is low in tone and menacing in tenor. The camera then pans back to show both the woman and the attendant as he looks painfully down at his injured hand, while the woman briefly displays a sadistic smile (see Figure 1 bottom).

There are three notable features in this brief sequence of actions: (a) scratching motion as parallel lines, (b) downward gesture and gaze and sound, and (c) scratching and parallel lines as symptoms of underlying, hidden psychic disturbances. We imaginatively simulate what it must be like to experience hand scratching, possibly from both the point of views of the actor and recipient. For example, we simulate the attendant's facial expression to understand something of what he may be feeling. We also view the patient's scratching, which stands in stark contrast to her prior sweet demeanor, as suggesting some psychological problem that made her behave in this manner, again given our embodied understandings of what sometimes motivates people's physical attacks against others. Our experience of the music is also guided by simulations related to the metaphorical theme that *down is bad, harmful, or menacing*.

One possible emerging metaphor from our observing this scene is *disturbing inner thoughts are harmful bodily actions*. Although this connection seems metonymical where one small event stands for a larger one (e.g., other symbolic acts of bodily harm), we still typically form a metaphorical understanding of the woman's mindset as if it were a type of outward harm body damage done to others. I do not claim that this is necessarily an entrenched conceptual metaphor, but it is an interpretation that some spectators may infer, even if partially and quite unconsciously. My own experience of watching SPELLBOUND immediately led me to quite consciously recognize that this little sequence of actions was both locally symbolic and potentially significant in understanding what was to follow in the film (i.e., the camera's specific, detailed looked at the hand scratching action, the

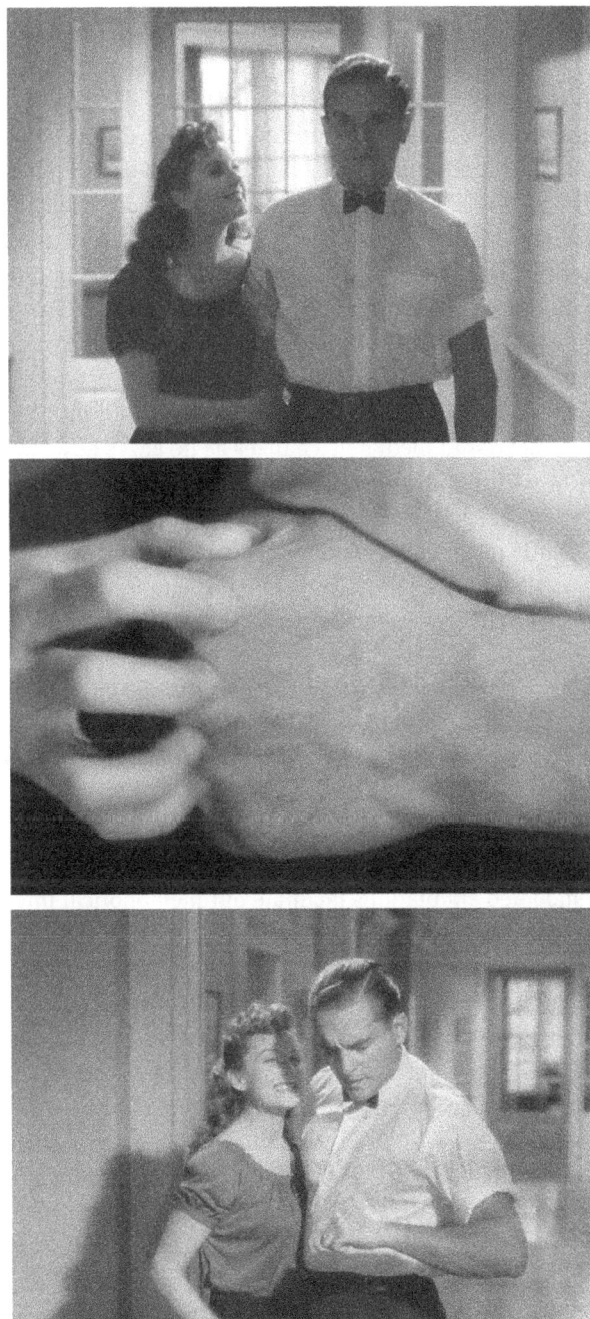

Figure 1: Hand scratching sequence in SPELLBOUND.

low tone music, and the patient's sadistic gleeful facial expression suggested this importance, even if the entire sequence lasted only a few seconds).

A second cinematic expressive movement in the film also occurs early on when the supposedly new medical director, Dr. Edwardes, is sitting in a formal dining room having lunch with Dr. Constance Peterson and others of his new colleagues. Up to this point, we have no idea that "the man posing as Edwardes is in actual fact John Ballantyne, who is suffering from severe amnesia and, not knowing who he is, believes he has killed the real Edwardes in order to steal his identity" (as Müller and Kappelhoff 2018, 207, summarize). But in this scene, a hint emerges, that this man is experiencing psychological difficulties. While he is listening to a colleague, he notices that the other person is emphasizing a point as he drags the tip of a fork across the table cloth in front of them (see Figure 2). His demeanor immediately changes as he gazes downward at the fork and table cloth, which is also accompanied by a downward movement in the music. The sequence, then, features four key elements: (a) downward gaze and implied downward movement in soundtrack, (b) fork movement as imprinting or scratching upon the body, (c) parallel lines represent harm to another person or body, and (d) split again between manifest and latent content in the character's personality.

Once again, spectators may tacitly, or quite consciously, recognize the metaphorical idea that *disturbing inner thoughts are harmful bodily actions*, or at least *disturbing inner thoughts are harmful bodily actions against other people and objects*. Note how this particular cinematic expressive movement in this scene elaborates upon the metaphorical sequences we observed only minutes before during the film, even if that scene involved different people and different actions.

Various embodied simulations facilitate our metaphorical interpretations of this scene. We imagine ourselves using the fork to make the marks on the table cloth, even sensing the specific degree of pressure required to create the scratches. But we also simulate the sensation of our own bodies being engraved in this way similar to how the attendant must have felt being scratch by the patient (and also doing so to create a set of parallel lines). Ballantyne's downward glance and facial expression are also interpreted in a bodily manner as we simulate what those actions must be like to experience in this particular context.

A third metaphorically orchestrated expressive movement immediately follows the preceding one. After gazing down at the parallel lines etched on the table cloth, the camera focuses on Ballantyne picking up a butter knife and subtly trying to erase the pattern from the cloth (see Figure 3). This small movement quickly evokes the metaphorical idea that by erasing the parallel lines scratched on the table, Ballantyne is attempting to ignore or eradicate the latent symbolic content related to these lines from his mind.

Figure 2: Fork engraving on table cloth (SPELLBOUND).

Figure 3: Attempted erasure of parallel lines (SPELLBOUND).

The specific metaphorical message here is *forgetting disturbing inner thoughts is erasing outward physical or bodily damage*. Note here how the attempted erasing of the parallel lines from the table cloth generally mimics the attendant's attempt to rub away the effect of the woman's fingernails scratching along the back of his hand in a parallel manner. Thus, spectators are already to see a build-up of cinematic expressive movements that convey roughly similar metaphorical ideas as they watch more and more of the film.

A fourth orchestrated expressive movement, which is linked to the earlier ones, occurs later in the film when Ballantyne and Dr. Petersen visit one of her older, now retired colleagues. They arrive at his residence and end up discussing one of Ballantyne's dreams (i.e., the Dalí sequence), one part of which involved a skiing scene that could be quite relevant to uncovering the underlying root of his phobia. Later on, Ballantyne and Petersen go upstairs to their guest room for the evening. As they were discussing where each of them will sleep, Ballantyne looks over at the bed and notices a cover with parallel lines as the pattern. Seeing this immediately causes Ballantyne to focus intensely on the bed cover (see Figure 4), again accompanied by a downward music score and a disturbed look on Ballantyne's face. Petersen notices this and begins to question Ballantyne, like a psychiatrist, but in a loving manner, to help Ballantyne recover the source of this psychologically disturbing image.

Figure 4: Observing parallel lines on bed cover (SPELLBOUND).

Again, we understand Ballantyne's facial expression in terms of our own embodied simulation processes, and recognize that he may be entranced by the bed cover because it possibly reminds him of some disturbing memory. The experimental literature on mirror neurons and perceptual recognition show that viewing a static object (e.g., bed cover) also affords actions associated with it, including those relevant to how the object was created (Gibbs 2006 for a review). "Some of the ways people infer causal influences on static objects must be due to their own previous, and anticipated future, actions against objects and the effects that occur thereafter" (Gibbs 2006, 57). When Ballantyne sees the parallel lines on the bed cover, he may be imaging how it was created (e.g., scratching hands, fork engravings on table cloths), but also other actions related to his past experiences of parallel lines, especially those in which the body has been damaged.

The film soon moves to a scene in which Ballantyne and Petersen are about to ski down a mountain side, as depicted in Figure 5, to recreate the part of the earlier described dream in an attempt to better understand its significance. Notice one subtle, but still highly relevant, feature of this image, which is that the skies and poles that the two of them are holding are all arranged as parallel lines within the shot. Parallel lines are presented as a critical, repetitive stylistic

Figure 5: Arriving at the top of the mountain (SPELLBOUND).

feature of the film. This repetition of the parallel lines image surely evokes our prior understanding of its metaphorical content with its embodied motivations (e.g., violations of the body or possibly standing for a past violation of the body – a metonymical inference).

Ballantyne and Petersen are soon skiing in a dramatic manner, with intense music playing in the background and the camera moving back and forth to each of their faces as they rush down the mountain side. Whenever the camera focuses on Ballantyne's face (Figure 6), one apprehends that he may not only be experiencing a perilous physical journey down the mountain, with a looming cliff edge below, but that he may be undergoing a difficult psychological journey as well, perhaps leading back to the buried memory that is the cause of his emotional disturbances (i.e., *searching for a memory in one's mind is a physical journey*). Petersen, who is also flying down the hill, constantly looks over at Ballantyne, almost as if she is still acting as a psychiatrist working with her patient even while skiing. Finally, Ballantyne seems to gain an awareness of something crystalizing in his mind (e.g., the widening of his eyes toward the end of the downhill sequence), which is surely relevant to his past traumatic reactions to certain disturbing stimuli (e.g., parallel lines).

Our Metaphorical Experiences of Film — 133

Figure 6: Skiing down the mountain (SPELLBOUND).

At the end of the scene, Ballantyne and Petersen come close to the edge of the mountain side, but do not fall over and simply collapse onto the ground into each other's arms (see Figure 7). Ballantyne and Petersen look quite scared, perhaps in recognition of the physical danger they just successfully avoided, yet there is also a visible relief in their faces because Ballantyne has finally recovered the troubling hidden memory. Hitchcock orchestrates this image in a stylized manner in which Ballantyne's and Petersen's skis and poles are no longer presented as a series of parallel lines but are arranged perpendicularly.

The obvious symbolic interpretation of this scene, which is in contrast to the earlier multimodal images, is that non-parallel skis represent escape from tyranny of parallel lines in the repressed mind. This psychological realization is, more generally, an embodied process as seen in the skiing downhill to a potentially dangerous, but ultimately survivable, location (i.e., *finding a sought after memory is arriving at desired location in a physical journey*). Our experience of this entire ski scene is quite visceral as if we were the people skiing rapidly downhill and facing great danger (e.g., skiing off the mountain or crashing). We feel the sensation of going fast, almost recklessly, down the mountain given our simulations

Figure 7: End of ski scene (SPELLBOUND).

of what this must be like for us, and having, perhaps, in the past experienced moments of sudden psychological revelation.

What was the recovered memory that tormented Ballantyne? As Ballantyne and Petersen sit in the snow, Ballantyne recounts the story of a childhood event, which is also depicted in several moving images on the screen (Figure 8). He is sitting on the top of a stoop or at the top of a series of downward steps leading from a house entrance to the street below. All one can see are Ballantyne's shoes at the time, with his little brother sitting with his back toward him at the bottom of the stoop. Notice also the fence, with its parallel railings, along the sidewalk to the left of where his younger brother sits. Suddenly, we see the moving image of Ballantyne's shoes sliding down the slope of the stoop quite rapidly and then making forceful contact with his brother's backside, sending him flying up into the air and landing violently on top of the pointed fence railings. The young boy is obviously, and quite disturbingly, killed.

Spectators of this horrible accident initially adopt Ballantyne's point-of-view as if we engaged in this bodily action leading to the boy's death. We also can quickly switch perspectives and simulate for ourselves what it must be like, in a deeply embodied manner, to be the younger brother, flying up in the air and slamming down on top of the fence railings. The moving image and accompanying downward music score of Ballantyne sliding down the stoop gives the embodied feel that *downward movement is bad*. Ballantyne then comments, again while still sitting on the mountain with Petersen, that he is responsible for his brother's death and admits to struggling over whether his action was accidental or not. There is some ambiguity, though, as to whether Ballantyne intended to harm his brother and we as spectators almost immediately begin to re-run the scene in our minds, via embodied simulation processes, to imagine for ourselves exactly how guilty Ballantyne should feel about what happened. Our ability to re-analyze film scenes in this manner and glean different interpretations from these re-imaginings shows another way in which embodied simulations shape our experiences of film.

There is an obvious metaphorical correspondence between the skiing sequence and the sequence of Ballantyne sliding down the stoop and causing his brother's death. Both sequences depict fast, downward movement, with congruent music scores. But these two journeys have different endings with one resulting in the achievement of a desired, abstract goal (e.g., retrieving a traumatic memory) and the other in tragedy (e.g., the young boy's death). One characterization of this metaphorical understanding is *remembering a traumatic event is a dangerous physical journey to a difficult to find location.*

Figure 8: Flashback to the brother's death (SPELLBOUND).

Conclusion

Films work to modulate our cognitive and affective experiences – they push us around in nuanced ways through orchestrated audiovisual moving images. Our experience of metaphorically orchestrated movements in films, such as SPELL-BOUND, are grounded in embodied simulation processes in which we imagine ourselves engaging in the multimodal events depicted. We understand these orchestrated movements not as discrete entities, but as unfolding cascades of thoughts and feelings over time as the film progresses. My argument has been that this build-up of metaphoricity arises from the confluence of embodied simulations.

Embodied simulations vary in richness, texture, degree of multimodality depending on many factors, such as who we are (i.e., our personal background and experiences, including those of watching films), our motivations and attentional focus when watching a film (i.e., casual viewing, pure entertainment, deeper scholarly analysis), and, of course, the specific multimodal images presented. These factors interact in complex ways to give film experience, including metaphorical film experience, great specificity. For these reasons, there may often be great within- and between-individual variation in the ways we experience and understand films. Experiences of specific metaphorical meanings in film dynamically ebb and flow, are often overlapping, and are not always complete and discreet. As we watch a specific film, we may build up more elaborated embodied simulations given what we have seen earlier in the film. Moreover, enriched embodied simulations are created from our prior viewings of the same film, or even films within the same genre.

Watching films, and the embodied simulation processes created during this activity, share many of the perceptual, cognitive, and emotional processes employed when we experience and interpret events in the real-world. Still, watching films is a distinct activity as are the ways embodied simulations operate in our film experiences. As Gallese and Guerra observe about embodied simulation and film viewing:

> When watching a movie, our embodied simulation becomes *liberated* because it is freed from the burden of modeling an actual presence in daily life. We find ourselves situated at a safe distance from what is being narrated on the screen and this magnifies our receptivity. Through an immersive state in which our attention is entirely focused on the narrated filmic world, we can fully deploy our simulative resources, letting our defensive guard against daily reality to slip for a while. (Gallese and Guerra 2012, 196)

Our film watching experiences, therefore, allow us to engage in a wide-ranging assortment of embodied simulation activities given that we are mere spectators and not participants in the scenes observed. This freedom to run enriched simulations provides one of the bases for why we are often immersed within the film world, which is again quite different in many ways from our typical observation of real-world events. Embodied simulations also provide the grounding for why we feel "moved" when watching films because being "moved" is not mere metaphor but correctly characterizes our sensory experience of being "pushed around" by audiovisual compositions that were designed for this purpose. We are not typically aware of these embodied simulation processes because they mostly operate automatically and unconsciously. Still, film spectators have some control over how embodied simulations unfold through changes in the physical situations in which we view films (e.g., the places, the device on which we watch them), who we watch them with, our in-the-moment motivations (e.g., casual entertainment, reflective scholarly analysis), and present bodily states (e.g., being hungry, tired, intoxicated). Even film-makers use embodied simulations in their creative processes. Consider Alfred Hitchcock's statement, "I have a strongly visual mind. I visualize a picture right down to the final cuts. I write all this out in the greatest detail in the script, and then I don't look at the script while I'm shooting." He is essentially noting the critical role that his imaginative simulations play in his writing, designing, and directing the production of his films.

Embodied conceptual metaphors or systematic metaphors may really be summary descriptions of the products of embodied simulation processes (Gibbs 2017). Common embodied, conceptual metaphors, such as LIFE IS A JOURNEY, UNDERSTANDING IS GRASPING, and KNOWING IS SEEING are really summary descriptions of the products of embodied simulation processes. Similarly, systematic metaphors, which capture more of the context-specific metaphoricity in linguistic and nonlinguistic domains (Cameron 2010, Cameron et al. 2009), may also be characterized as summary descriptions of the emergent simulation products of film viewing. One implication of studying people's experiences of multimodal metaphor in films as orchestrated, dynamic movements is that it properly emphasizes the embodied, sensory, and always unfolding nature of metaphorical experience.

Audiovisual sources

SPELLBOUND, Alfred Hitchcock, Selznick International Pictures, USA 1945.

Bibliography

Beattie, Geoffrey, and Laura Sale. 2012. "Do Metaphoric Gestures Influence how a Message is Perceived? The Effects of Metaphoric Gesture-Speech Matches and Mismatches on Semantic Communication and Social Judgment." *Semiotica* 192: 77–98.

Bergen, Benjamin. 2012. *Louder Than Words. The New Science of how the Mind Makes Meaning.* New York: Basic Books.
Boroditsky, Lera, and Michael Ramscar. 2002. "The Roles of Body and Mind in Abstract Thought." *Psychological Science* 13 (2): 185–189.
Cameron, Lynne. 2010. "The Discourse Dynamics Framework for Metaphor." In *Metaphor Analysis. Research Practice in Applied Linguistics, Social Sciences and the Humanities*, edited by Lynne Cameron and Robert Maslen, 77–96. London: Equinox.
Cameron, Lynne, Robert Maslen, Zazie Todd, John Maule, Peter Stratton, and Neil Stanley. 2009. "The Discourse Dynamics Approach to Metaphor and Metaphor-led Discourse Analysis." *Metaphor & Symbol* 24: 1–27.
Cienki, Alan, and Cornelia Müller, eds. 2008. *Metaphor and Gesture*. Amsterdam: John Benjamins.
Citron, Francesca, and Adele Goldberg. 2014. "Social Context Modulates the Effect of Hot Temperature on Perceived Interpersonal Warmth. A Study of Embodied Metaphors." *Language and Cognition* 6 (1): 1–11.
Crowther, Bosley. 1945. "Movie Review – SPELLBOUND." *The New York Times*, 2 November 1945, 22.
Desai, Rutvik, Jeffrey Binder, Lisa Conant, Quintino Mano, and Michael Seidenberg. 2011. "The Neural Career of Sensory-Motor Metaphors." *Journal of Cognitive Neuroscience* 23 (9): 2376–2386.
Forceville, Charles, and Eduardo Urios-Aparisi, eds. 2009. *Multimodal Metaphor*. Berlin: Mouton de Gruyter.
Gallese, Vittorio, and Michelle Guerra. 2012. "Embodying Movies. Embodied Simulation and Film Studies." *Journal of Philosophy and the Moving Image* 3: 183–210.
Gibbs, Raymond. 2006. *Embodiment and Cognitive Science*. New York: Cambridge University Press.
Gibbs, Raymond W. Jr. 1994. *The Poetics of Mind. Figurative Thought, Language, and Understanding*. Cambridge: Cambridge University Press.
Gibbs, Raymond W. Jr. 2017. *Metaphor Wars. Conceptual Metaphor in Human Life*. New York: Cambridge University Press.
Glenberg, Arthur, and Michael Kaschak. 2002. "Grounding Language in Action." *Psychonomic Bulletin & Review* 9 (3): 58–565.
Glenberg, Arthur, Marc Sato, Luigi Cattaneo, Lucia Riggio, Daniele Palumbo, and Giovanni G. Buccino. 2008. "Processing Abstract Language Modulates Motor System Activity." *Quarterly Journal of Experimental Psychology* 61 (6): 905–919.
Grafton, Stephen. 2011. "Embodied Cognition and the Simulation of Action to Understand Others." *Annals of the New York Academy of Sciences* 1156: 97–117.
Kappelhoff, Hermann, and Cornelia Müller. 2011. "Embodied Meaning Construction. Multimodal Metaphor and Expressive Movement in Speech, Gesture, and Feature Film." *Metaphor and the Social World* 1 (2): 121–153.
MacDougall, Douglas. 2006. *The Corporeal Image. Film, Ethnography, and the Senses*. Princeton: Princeton University Press.
Müller, Cornelia, and Hermann Kappelhoff. 2018. *Cinematic Metaphor. Experience – Affectivity – Temporality*. In collaboration with Sarah Greifenstein, Dorothea Horst, Thomas Scherer, and Christina Schmitt. Berlin/Boston: Walter de Gruyter.
Müller, Cornelia, and Christina Schmitt. 2015. "Audio-Visual Metaphors of the Financial Crisis. Meaning Making and the Flow of Experience." *Revista Brasileira de Linguística Aplicada* 15 (2): 311–342.

N.N. 1945. "SPELLBOUND – Review." *Harrsion's Reports*, 3 November 1945, 175.
Pulvermüller, Friedemann. 2013. "How Neurons Make Meaning. Brain Mechanisms for Embodied and Abstract-Symbolic Semantics." *Trends in Cognitive Sciences* 17 (9): 458–470.
Santana, Eduardo, and Manuel de Vega. 2011. "Metaphors are Embodied, and so are their Literal Counterparts." *Frontiers in Psychology* 2 (90): 1–12.
Schippers, Marleen, Alard Roebroeck, Remco Renken, Luca Nanetti, and Christian Keysers. 2010. "Mapping the Information Flow from one Brain to Another During Gestural Communication." *Proceedings of the National Academy of Science* 107 (20): 9388–9393.
Schmitt, Christina, Sarah Greifenstein, and Hermann Kappelhoff. 2014. "Expressive Movement and Metaphoric Meaning Making in Audio-Visual Media." In *Body – Language – Communication. An International Handbook on Multimodality in Human Interaction*, edited by Cornelia Müller, Alan Cienki, Ellen Fricke, Silva H. Ladewig, David McNeill, and Jana Bressem, 2092–2112. Berlin/Boston: De Gruyter Mouton.
Shimamura, Art, and Stephen Palmer, eds. 2012. *Aesthetic Science. Connecting Minds, Brains, and Experience*. New York: Oxford University Press.
Truffaut, François. 1983. *Hitchcock/Truffaut*. New York: Simon & Shuster.
Wilson, Nicole, and Raymond W. Gibbs, Jr. 2007. "Real and Imagined Body Movement Primes Metaphor Comprehension." *Cognitive Science* 31: 721–731.

Name Index

Alibali, Martha W. 60
Anderson, Barbara Fisher 74
Anderson, John R. 74
Anderson, Joseph D. 69, 74–75
Armstrong, David F. 63
Assayas, Olivier 23

Barker, Jennifer 12
Barlow, Michael 54
Bateman, John 2
Beattie, Geoffrey 125
Benjamin, Walter 111
Bergen, Benjamin K. 60, 124
Bergman, Ingrid 120
Bergs, Alexander 55
Berry, Jo 32
Black, Max 2–4, 12
Bleibtreu, Moritz 81
Blumenberg, Hans 3, 12, 14, 93–118
Boroditsky, Lera 124
Branigan, Edward 43
Bressem, Jana 58
Budd, Mike 41
Buñuel, Luis 46

Cameron, Lynne 4–7, 12–13, 17–34, 138
Carter, Ronald 54
Certeau, Michel de 72, 108
Chafe, Wallace 18, 57
Chernigovskaya, Tatyana Vladimirovna 62
Choe, Steve 38
Chomsky, Noam 54, 57, 62
Cienki, Alan 12–14, 53–65, 70–71, 121
Citron, Francesca 125
Clark, Herbert H. 56, 61
Coëgnarts, Maarten 2, 75, 78
Crosby, Bing 117
Crowther, Bosley 121

Dalí, Salvador 23, 120, 130
Davis, Bette 21
Deignan, Alice 22–26
Deleuze, Gilles 2

Desai, Rutvik 125
Doty, Mark 20
Du Bois, John W. 54
Dudley, Andrew 38, 41

Eisenstein, Sergej 46
Eisner, Lotte H. 43–46
Elsaesser, Thomas 36
Eusterschulte, Anne 12, 14, 93–118

Fahlenbrach, Kathrin 2, 12, 14, 69–89
Fillmore, Charles J. 55
Fisher, Daniel 93
Forceville, Charles 2, 75, 78, 121
Foucault, Michel 111
Freud, Sigmund 38
Fricke, Ellen 55, 59

Gallese, Vittorio 123, 137
Geeraerts, Dirk 54
Gehring, Petra 12
Gibbs, Raymond W. Jr. 3, 12–15, 24–25, 60, 63, 77–78, 120–138
Glenberg, Arthur 124–125
Goldberg, Adele 125
Goldstein, Bruce 74–76
Grafton, Stephen 124
Greifenstein, Sarah 1–15, 70–73, 122–123
Grodal, Torben K. 69, 74–75
Guerra, Michelle 123, 137
Gutierrez Marquez, José Mario 12

Harder, Susanne 79
Harris, Randy A. 54
Hausman, Carl R. 60
Heaney, Seamus 20
Henry, Michael 36
Hitchcock, Alfred 12–15, 23, 93–118, 120, 121, 133, 138
Horst, Dorothea 1–15, 70
Hostetter, Autumn B. 60

Iriskhanova, Olga 60
Iverson, Jana M. 61

Jakobson, Roman 13, 37, 57, 63
Jensen, Thomas Wiben 3
Johnson, Mark 3–4, 12, 26, 63, 74, 77–78

Kant, Immanuel 60
Kaplan, E. Ann 37
Kappelhoff, Hermann 1–15, 17, 21–22, 30, 41–46, 50–51, 53, 70–75, 80–81, 87, 94, 122–125, 128
Kaschak, Michael 124
Kemmer, Suzanne 54
Kendon, Adam 57
Kittay, Eva Feder 18
Koppe, Simo 79
Kövecses, Zóltan 78, 84
Kracauer, Siegfried 40
Kravanja, Peter 2, 75, 78

Lacan, Jacques 38
Ladewig, Silva H. 55
Lakoff, George 3–4, 12, 26, 63, 74, 78
Lang, Fritz 36
Langacker, Ronald W. 54–55
Larsen-Freeman, Diane 18, 25
Leddy, Thomas 58
Levy, Elena T. 55
Light, Andrew 58
Linell, Per 18, 54
Lingford, Ruth 12
Lucas, George 76

MacDougall, Douglas 123
Magee, Patrick 32
Marghetis, Tyler 60
Marks, Laura 69
Maslen, Robert 23–24
McCarthy, Michael 54
McNeill, David 55–56
Merleau-Ponty, Maurice 4, 56
Metz, Christian 13, 37–39, 46
Müller, Cornelia 1–15, 17, 21–22, 30, 41–46, 50–51, 53, 58–59, 64, 70–75, 79–81, 87, 94, 121–125, 128
Murnau, Friedrich Wilhelm 13, 36–51

Nannicelli, Ted 74
Naremore, James 37

Palmer, Stephen 123
Payne, Alexander 22
Pearson, Roberta E. 46
Peck, Gregory 120
Plantinga, Carl 69, 74
Potente, Franka 81
Pragglejaz 23
Pulvermüller, Friedemann 124

Ramscar, Michael 124
Rilke, Rainer Maria 93, 107–110
Rinsch, Carl Erik 8
Robison, Arthur 37
Ropars-Wuilleumier, Marie-Claire 36
Rosch, Eleanor 55

Sadowski, Piotr 41
Saito, Yuriko 60
Sale, Laura 125
Samosata, Lucian of 112
Santana, Eduardo 125
Sartre, Jean Paul 110
Scherer, Thomas 1–15, 70
Scheunemann, Dietrich 41
Schippers, Marleen 125
Schmitt, Christina 1–15, 70, 73, 122–123
Schoonjans, Steven 55
Shaviro, Steven 69
Shimamura, Arthur 123
Shklovskiy, Viktor 57–60
Sinnerbrink, Robert 45
Smith, Greg M. 69, 74
Smith, Jonathan M. 58
Sobchack, Vivian 4, 12, 69, 72
Steen, Francis 64
Stern, Daniel N. 79
Sterne, Laurence 114
Stokoe, William C. 63
Streeck, Jürgen 58
Swain, Merrill 19
Sweetser, Eve 59

Taberham, Paul 74
Tannen, Deborah 62
Taylor, Jim 22
Thelen, Esther 61
Tong, Yao 59

Truffaut, François 120–121
Turner, Mark 63–64, 74
Tykwer, Tom 12, 14, 70, 81

Urios-Aparisi, Eduardo 2, 75, 78, 121

Vaever, Mette 79
Vega, Manuel de 125

Wedel, Michael 11–13, 36–51
Whittock, Trevor 2, 36, 39

Wiene, Robert 36
Wilcox, Sherman E. 63
Wildfeuer, Janina 2
Williams, Linda 36
Wilson, Nicole 124
Wu, Suwei 64
Wyler, William 12, 21, 24, 72

Zima, Elisabeth 55

Subject Index

Actio per distans 14, 93–118
Aesthetics
- aesthetic attention 14, 53, 60–63
- aesthetics of audiovisual images 5, 10, 42, 70–73, 89
Affect
- affect modulation 6–7, 13, 41, 43, 71, 81, 137
- affective/interaffective dynamics 6, 69–70, 79
- affective resonance 43, 50, 76, 94
- poetics of affect 42–45, 50
As-if (mode) 58–59, 64, 72, 124, 126, 132–135
Audiovisual representation 2, 11, 13, 36, 39, 40–43, 71–75, 97, 111

Cinematic expressivity 4–7, 13–14, 18, 36–51, 70–74, 80–81, 87, 122–136
Cognitive sciences 6, 15, 62, 69, 76, 123–125
Conceptualization 14, 54–55, 60, 95–97

Dynamics of film and discourse 2, 5–7, 13, 18–25, 28, 32–33, 53–55, 71, 79, 123

Embodiment
- embodied experience 1, 6–7, 11, 71–77, 87, 124, 135 (see also Experience; Reflexivity of feeling)
- embodied simulation 15, 121–128, 131, 135–138
- image schema 77–81, 89
Emotion 7, 12, 43, 45, 79, 84, 107–108, 115, 120–121, 132, 137
Experience
- affective experience 5–7, 41, 43, 46, 63, 72–76, 137
- embodied experience 2–7, 11, 74–77, 87, 124 (see also Embodiment)
- interaffective experience (see Interaffectivity)
- intersubjective experience 1 (see also Intersubjectivity)

Expressive movement 4–7, 12–14, 17–18, 21, 23, 25, 36–51, 70–74, 80–81, 87, 121, 122–136

Film and media studies
- cognitive film and media studies 4, 69, 74–75
- film historiography 3–5, 13, 36, 41–42
- film theory 4–5, 13, 36–37, 41–42

Genre 4, 13, 25, 36, 39, 42–43, 46, 50, 75, 78, 137
Gestalt
- cross-modal gestalt 79–81, 85
- multidimensional experiential gestalt 3
Gesture
- gesture in face-to-face interaction 1, 5–7, 13–14, 45–46, 53–63, 70–73, 79, 121, 125
- gesture in film/audiovisual media 1, 6–7, 14, 45–46, 49, 53–65, 75, 122, 126
- gestural modes of representation 58–59, 62–65

Historicity of meaning-making 3, 5, 13, 18, 46, 95–98

Image schema 77–81, 89. See also Embodiment
Interaction
- face-to-face interaction 1–7, 13, 17–32, 38, 53–62, 70–71, 124
- interaction between spectators and film 6, 69–72, 87, 117, 123
Interaffectivity 70–71, 74, 79
Intersubjectivity 4–7

Language use 13, 54–57, 63
Life-world 94–100, 107, 109, 117
Linguistics
- applied linguistics 1, 12
- cognitive linguistics 1–2, 12, 14, 53–55, 62–63, 77
- generative linguistics 54, 61
- psycholinguistics 15, 124–125

Meaning-making 2–7, 12–15, 22, 72
Media specificity of audiovisual images 1–5, 69–70, 137
Metaphor
– audiovisual metaphor 2, 14, 70, 74–81, 89
– cinematic metaphor 1–15, 17–18, 21–22, 25, 29–34, 37, 41–42, 45–46, 50–51, 53–65, 70–73
– conceptual metaphor 3, 17, 20, 24, 28, 31, 33, 54, 78, 123, 126, 138
– 'doing' metaphor 2–6
– metaphor formulation 3–4, 13, 17–18, 24–34
– multimodal metaphor (face-to-face interaction) 2, 5–7, 53, 59, 71, 121
– multimodal metaphor (film) 2, 121, 138
– systematic metaphor 7, 13, 23–33, 138
Metaphor theories/approaches to metaphor
– cognitive approaches to metaphor in audiovisual images 3, 14, 70, 74–75, 81
– conceptual metaphor theory 3, 20, 28, 33, 54
– discourse dynamics approach to metaphor 5, 18–21, 25
– dynamic view of metaphor 1, 4
– metaphorology 3, 14, 93–118
– metonymy 29, 36–38, 41–42, 46, 63, 126, 132
– mode of experience/mode of perception 2–6, 97

– movement-image 1–7, 11, 14, 17, 22, 81
– traditional approaches to cinematic metaphor 2, 13, 36, 39
– transdisciplinary framework of cinematic metaphor 1–5, 8, 12–15, 41, 45–46, 50, 70
Multimodality
– (articulatory) modalities 2, 5, 13, 23, 32–33, 36, 38, 40–45, 57, 70–71, 76–77, 121, 123
– multimodal metaphor (see Metaphor)

Narrative 2, 13, 23, 32–33, 36, 38, 40–45, 76–77, 121

Phenomenology 56, 100, 110
– neo-phenomenological film theory 4, 69–70, 110
Poetics 14, 19, 27, 39, 42–45, 50, 53, 57–63, 117
Poiesis
– poiesis of film-viewing 2, 5–7, 14, 94, 117
– poiesis of metaphorizing 20, 27
– reflexivity of feeling 4–6 (see also Embodiment)
– rhetoric 3, 94–97, 101, 107, 117
– situatedness of meaning 3–6, 95
– temporality 3, 5, 7–8, 12, 14, 17, 56, 94, 97–98, 102, 107, 117

About the Authors

Lynne Cameron is a contemporary painter and Professor Emerita (previously Professor of Applied Linguistics) at the Open University, UK. From 2015 to 2017, she was Artist in Residence and Senior Fellow at *Cinepoetics*, Center for Advanced Film Studies at Freie Universität Berlin, where she explored metaphorical connections between the poiesis of film and of painting. Her artwork can be seen at www.lynnecameron.com. She is Founder Chair of the international Association for Researching and Applying Metaphor/RaAM. Cameron's academic career includes substantial research into the dynamics of metaphor in talk, which led to questioning established cognitive theories and to a range of theoretical and methodological contributions to metaphor studies, set out in journal articles, chapters, and books, including *Metaphor Analysis* (Equinox 2010, co-edited with R. Maslen), *Metaphor and Reconciliation* (Routledge 2011), and *Complex Systems and Applied Linguistics* (Oxford University Press 2008, co-authored with D. Larsen-Freeman). From 2008 to 2012, she held a *Global Uncertainties* Research Fellowship, funded by the UK Economic and Social Research Council, leading a research project into empathy in post-conflict situations. The e-book *Empathy Dynamics in Conflict Transformation* and other publications from this project are available at: wels.open.ac.uk/research/centres/creet/research-themes/languages-and-applied-linguistics/completed-projects/edict

Alan Cienki is Professor of Language Use and Cognition at the Vrije Universiteit/VU in Amsterdam, the Netherlands, where he has worked since 2006. He also holds a part-time appointment as Professor at Moscow State Linguistic University in the Russian Federation where he founded and directs the Multimodal Communication and Cognition Lab, known in Russian as PoliMod. Previously he worked at Emory University, Atlanta, USA in the Graduate Institute of the Liberal Arts, the Program in Linguistics (which he co-founded), and the Department of Russian and East Asian Languages and Cultures. His research is based in cognitive linguistics, with a focus in recent years on spoken language and gesture. He is the author of *Ten Lectures on Spoken Language and Gesture from the Perspective of Cognitive Linguistics* (Brill 2017) and a co-editor of *Metaphor and Gesture* (Benjamins 2008) and of the two-volume handbook *Body – Language – Communication* (Mouton De Gruyter 2013, 2014). His research projects have been funded by grants from the Netherlands Organization for Scientific Research (NWO), the Netherlands Institute for Advanced Study, the Russian Science Foundation, and the German Academic Exchange Service. Cienki is a former Chair of the international Association for Researching and Applying Metaphor/RaAM and former Vice President of the International Society for Gesture Studies/ISGS. In 2016, Cienki was Senior Fellow at *Cinepoetics*, Center for Advanced Film Studies at Freie Universität Berlin.

Anne Eusterschulte (Dr. phil.) is Professor for History of Philosophy at the Department for Humanities at the Freie Universität Berlin (Germany). Her research includes history of philosophy from a longue durée perspective, transcultural conceptualizations of episteme, medieval and early modern philosophy with an emphasis on theories of imagination, the transfer of ancient philosophy, transcultural philologies and critical theory. Many of her studies are situated in the overlapping area of aesthetics, rhetorics and poetics. She is member of several transdisciplinary collaborative research centers, for instance, board member of the *Friedrich Schlegel Graduate School for Literary Studies*, of the CRC 980 *Episteme in Motion*, of the *Forum Middle Ages – Renaissance – Early Modern Period* and of the *Center for Aristotelian*

Studies (all Berlin). As Associated Researcher she partakes in the Centers for Advanced Studies *BildEvidenz. History and Aesthetics* and *Cinepoetics*. She has published in the fields of theory of images (*Zur Erscheinung kommen: Bildlichkeit als theoretischer Prozess*, co-ed. W.-M. Stock, Meiner 2016), history of ideas (*Gratia. Mediale und diskursive Konzeptualisierungen ästhetischer Erfahrung in der Vormoderne*, co-ed. U. Schneider, Harrassowitz 2018), and politics and aesthetics (*Videographierte Zeugenschaft: Ein interdisziplinärer Dialog*. co-ed. S. Knopp/S. Schulze, Velbrück Wissenschaft 2015).

Kathrin Fahlenbrach (Dr. phil.) is Professor for Film- and Media Studies at the Department for Media and Communication at the University of Hamburg (Germany). Her main research focus lies on cognitive film and media theory, embodiment and moving images and cognitive metaphors in audiovisual media; furthermore, she works on visual performances and the role of visual media in protest movements. She is author of several publications on audiovisual metaphors in moving images. In her book *Audiovisuelle Metaphern. Zur Körper- und Affektästhetik in Film und Fernsehen* (Schüren 2010) she offers a theoretical framework on embodied and emotion metaphors in audiovisual mass media. Recent articles include "Audiovisual Metaphors and Metonymies of Emotions and Depression in Moving Images" (Ervas/Gola/Rossi, De Gruyter 2017) and "Sonic Spaces in Movies: Audiovisual Metaphors and Embodied Meanings in Sound Design" (Wöllner, Routledge 2017). She has edited several volumes and is co-editor of an international book series at Berghahn Books. Lately she edited the volume *Embodied Metaphors in Film, Television, and Video Games: Cognitive Approaches* (Routledge 2016). She is board member of the *Society for the Cognitive Study of the Moving Image* (SCSMI). In 2016, Fahlenbrach was Senior Fellow at *Cinepoetics*, Center for Advanced Film Studies at Freie Universität Berlin.

Raymond W. Gibbs, Jr. is a cognitive scientist and former Distinguished Professor of Psychology at the University of California, Santa Cruz, USA. His research interests focus on embodied cognition, pragmatics, and figurative language. With issues that cross-cut disciplines, his works bridge experimental research with linguistics and cognitive sciences more generally. He is the author of several books about people's use and understanding of figurative language and the role of embodied experience in thought and language, such as *The Poetics of Mind: Figurative Thought, Language and Understanding* (1994), *Intentions in the Experience of Meaning* (1999), *Embodiment and Cognitive Science* (2006), *Interpreting Figurative Meaning* (2012, with H.L. Colston) and *Metaphor Wars. Conceptual Metaphors in Human Life* (2017), all published by Cambridge University Press. Among his edited volumes are *Irony in Language and Thought. A Cognitive Science Reader* (Earlbaum 2007, with H.L. Colston), the *Cambridge Handbook of Metaphor and Thought* (Cambridge University Press 2008), and *Mixing Metaphors* (John Benjamins 2016). He is editor of the journal *Metaphor and Symbol*. In 2016, Gibbs was Senior Fellow at *Cinepoetics*, Center for Advanced Film Studies at Freie Universität Berlin.

Michael Wedel (Dr. phil.) is Professor for Media History in the Digital Age at the Film University Babelsberg KONRAD WOLF, Germany, and co-director of *Cinepoetics – Center for Advanced Film Studies* (with H. Kappelhoff). His research focuses on German and international film history, the aesthetics of film and TV series as well as the poetics of genre (among others: musical film, Hollywood war film, and fantastic film). His book *Filmgeschichte als Krisengeschichte. Schnitte und Spuren durch den deutschen Film* (transcript 2011), offers a unique perspective on German cinema as a history of crisis formations. Since 1996, he has authored and edited numerous other books on film history and cinema aesthetics. His most recent publications include: *Körper, Tod und Technik. Metamorphosen des Kriegsfilms* (Konstanz University Press 2016, with Thomas Elsaesser), *Special Effects in der Wahrnehmung des Publikums* (Springer VS 2016, ed.), and *'So etwas Ähnliches wie Wahrheit'. Zugänge zu Thomas Harlan* (edition text+kritik 2017, ed. with J. Jockenhövel), and *Pictorial Affects, Senses of Rupture. On the Poetics and Culture of Popular German Cinema, 1910–1930* (forthcoming, 2019). He is also co-editor of the book series "Film, Fernsehen, Medienkultur" at Springer VS (with J. Eder, L. Mikos and C. Wegener) and of the Cinepoetics book series at De Gruyter (with H. Kappelhoff). Wedel is a founding directorial board member of the Brandenburg Centre for Media Studies (ZeM).

About the Editors

Sarah Greifenstein is Assistant Professor for Media, Culture and Communication at European University Viadrina in Frankfurt/Oder (Germany). From 2009 to 2013 she was junior researcher in the project "Multimodal Metaphor and Expressive Movement" headed by H. Kappelhoff and C. Müller at the interdisciplinary research center *Languages of Emotion* (Berlin). She is author of the book *Tempi der Bewegung – Modi des Gefühls. Expressivität, heitere Affekte und die Screwball Comedy* (de Gruyter forthcoming/2019). Beyond other publications, she is co-author of chapters for *Body – Language – Communication* (Mouton De Gruyter 2014), including "The discovery of the acting body" and "Expressive movement and metaphoric meaning making in audio-visual media". Together with H. Kappelhoff, she published various German and English articles on metaphor and embodiment. She is collaborating author of *Cinematic Metaphor. Experience – Affectivity – Temporality* (C. Müller/H. Kappelhoff, De Gruyter 2018). Greifenstein's research foci are the relation of audiovisual media and language, embodiment and audiovisual communication, the cultural-historical formation of poetics of affect, and metaphorical meaning constitution in audiovisual media.

Dorothea Horst is a postdoctoral researcher at the chair for Language Use and Multimodal Communication at European University Viadrina, Frankfurt/Oder (Germany). She works on intersubjectivity and the experiential dynamics of (figurative) meaning-making in multimodal interaction and audiovisual media. From 2009 to 2013 she was junior researcher in the project "Multimodal Metaphor and Expressive Movement" headed by H. Kappelhoff and C. Müller at the interdisciplinary research center *Languages of Emotion* (Berlin). In her PhD research *Meaning-Making and Political Campaign Advertising. A Cognitive-Linguistic and Film-Analytical Perspective on Audiovisual Figurativity* (De Gruyter 2018), she has explored the meaning-making role of metaphor and metonymy in German and Polish campaign commercials. Horst is co-author of the book chapter "Gesture as interactive expressive movement: Inter-affectivity in face-to-face communication" (*Body – Language – Communication*, Mouton De Gruyter 2014) and collaborating author of *Cinematic Metaphor. Experience – Affectivity – Temporality* (C. Müller/H. Kappelhoff, De Gruyter 2018).

Hermann Kappelhoff is Professor of Film Studies at Freie Universität Berlin (Germany), where he also co-directs the Center for Advanced Film Studies *Cinepoetics* (with M. Wedel). Following his research in the history, theory, and analysis of film and audiovisual media, he initiated numerous interdisciplinary projects involving cultural studies, philosophy, aesthetics, literature, fine arts, linguistics, and psychology, and developed various research projects and key activities at Freie Universität Berlin. He was principal investigator (2007–2014) and director (2010–2014) of the interdisciplinary research center *Languages of Emotion* (Berlin). In the Council of the German Research Foundation he represented Media Studies (2007–2015). He was a Max-Kade Visiting Professor at Vanderbilt University in Nashville, TN USA (2009/2010) and is Associate Researcher at the Center for Advanced Studies *BildEvidenz. History and Aesthetics*. Kappelhoff is the author of several books, among them *Matrix der Gefühle. Das Kino, das Melodrama und das Theater der Empfindsamkeit* (Vorwerk 8 2004), *The Politics and Poetics of Cinematic Realism* (Columbia University Press 2015), *Front Lines of Community: Hollywood Between War and Democracy* (De Gruyter 2018), and *Kognition und Reflexion. Zur Theorie filmischen Denkens* (De Gruyter 2018). Kappelhoff is co-author of *Cinematic Metaphor. Experience – Affectivity – Temporality* (with C. Müller, de Gruyter 2018). For further information: www.hermann-kappelhoff.de

https://doi.org/10.1515/9783110615036-011

About the Editors

Cornelia Müller is Professor of Language Use and Multimodal Communication at European University Viadrina, Frankfurt/Oder (Germany). She has published on multimodal forms of language use, focusing on gesture as an expressive medium (motivation and conventionalization), on embodied processes of multimodal communication, and on the experiential dynamics of metaphoric meaning in speech, gesture, and audiovisual media. She launched and edited the journal *Gesture* and the book series *Gesture Studies* (until 2010, with A. Kendon). She is editor-in-chief of *Body – Language – Communication. An international Handbook on Multimodality in Human Interaction* (De Gruyter 2013, 2014). From 2007 to 2013 she was principal investigator at the interdisciplinary research center Languages of Emotion (Freie Universität Berlin). As a Senior Fellow of *Cinepoetics*, Center for Advanced Film Studies at Freie Universität Berlin, she co-directed the center's work on 'Film Images, Cinematic Thinking, and Cognition' (2015/2016, with H. Kappelhoff and M. Wedel). Her books include *Redebegleitende Gesten* (Spitz 1998), *Metaphors, Dead and Alive, Sleeping and Waking. A Dynamic View* (UoC Press 2008), and the edited volume *Metaphor and Gesture* (Benjamins 2008, with A. Cienki). Müller is co-author of *Cinematic Metaphor. Experience – Affectivity – Temporality* (De Gruyter 2018, with H. Kappelhoff) and is currently preparing a textbook on gesture and language (Routledge, to appear, with J. Bressem and S.H. Ladewig).

Thomas Scherer is *Cinepoetics* doctoral student (working title: *Audiovisual Persuasion. Aggressive Metaphors and Feel-Bad-Movies*) and junior researcher in the digital-humanities project *Audiovisual Rhetorics of Affect* funded by the German Federal Ministry of Education and Research (BMBF) situated at the Freie Universität Berlin and the Hasso Plattner Institute Potsdam (Germany). From 2009 to 2013 he was student assistant in the project "Multimodal Metaphor and Expressive Movement" headed by H. Kappelhoff and C. Müller at the interdisciplinary research center *Languages of Emotion* (Berlin). He is co-author of the book chapter "Expressive Movements in Audiovisual Media. Modulating Affective Experience" (*Body – Language – Communication*, Mouton De Gruyter 2014) and collaborating author of *Cinematic Metaphor. Experience – Affectivity – Temporality* (C. Müller/H. Kappelhoff, De Gruyter 2018). Scherer's research foci are the aesthetics of utility films and TV news, digital research methods in film studies, as well as audiovisual rhetorics and metaphors.

Christina Schmitt is postdoctoral researcher at *Cinepoetics*, Center for Advanced Film Studies at the Freie Universität Berlin (Germany). From 2009 to 2013 she was junior researcher in the project "Multimodal Metaphor and Expressive Movement" headed by H. Kappelhoff and C. Müller at the interdisciplinary research center *Languages of Emotion* (Berlin). She is author of the book *Wahrnehmen, fühlen, verstehen. Metaphorisieren und audiovisuelle Bilder* (De Gruyter forthcoming/2019) and collaborating author of *Cinematic Metaphor. Experience – Affectivity – Temporality* (C. Müller/H. Kappelhoff, De Gruyter 2018). In *Building Bridges for Multimodal Research* (Peter Lang 2015) she published the chapter "Embodied Meaning making in audio-visuals. First steps toward a notion of mode". For *Body – Language – Communication* (Mouton De Gruyter 2014), she is co-author of several chapters focussing on affectivity, embodiment and meaning-making in film and in face-to-face interaction. Furthermore, she is co-editor of *Metaphor in the Arts, in Media and Communication* (*mediaesthetics* No. 2 (2017), with M. Grotkopp) and *Emotionen. Ein interdisziplinäres Handbuch* (Metzler forthcoming/2019, with H. Kappelhoff/J.-H. Bakels/H. Lehmann). Schmitt's research on film and audiovisual media focuses on cinematic expressivity, embodiment, performativity, temporality and metaphorical meaning constitution.

www.ingramcontent.com/pod-product-compliance
Lightning Source LLC
Chambersburg PA
CBHW050112170426
43198CB00014B/2545